The Emeritus Professor:
Old Rank - New Meaning

by James E. Mauch, Jack W. Birch, and Jack Matthews

ASHE-ERIC Higher Education Report 2, 1990

Prepared by

*Clearinghouse on Higher Education
The George Washington University*

In cooperation with

*Association for the Study
of Higher Education*

Published by

*School of Education and Human Development
The George Washington University*

Jonathan D. Fife, Series Editor

Cite as

Mauch, James E., Jack W. Birch, and Jack Matthews. *The Emeritus Professor: Old Rank - New Meaning.* ASHE-ERIC Higher Education Report No. 2. Washington, D.C.: School of Education and Human Development, The George Washington University, 1990.

Library of Congress Catalog Card Number 90-060888
ISSN 0884-0040
ISBN 0-9623882-9-7

Managing Editor: Bryan Hollister
Manuscript Editor: Eileen M. O'Brien
Cover design by Michael David Brown, Rockville, Maryland

The ERIC Clearinghouse on Higher Education invites individuals to submit proposals for writing monographs for the *ASHE-ERIC Higher Education Report* series. Proposals must include:
1. A detailed manuscript proposal of not more than five pages.
2. A chapter-by-chapter outline.
3. A 75-word summary to be used by several review committees for the initial screening and rating of each proposal.
4. A vita and a writing sample.

ERIC Clearinghouse on Higher Education
School of Education and Human Development
The George Washington University
One Dupont Circle, Suite 630
Washington, DC 20036-1183

This publication was prepared partially with funding from the Office of Educational Research and Improvement, U.S. Department of Education, under contract no. ED RI-88-062014. The opinions expressed in this report do not necessarily reflect the positions or policies of OERI or the Department.

EXECUTIVE SUMMARY

What Prompts an Interest in the Emeritus Status?

The new view of the emeritus professorship has important policy implications throughout higher education. The changes in progress regarding emeritus status are only beginning to be recognized nationally, though examples can be found on campuses in many states. Moreover, the changes take on special relevance for higher education planning now, when the emeritus rank may be converging with institutional practices, particularly those connected with tenure, retirement, benefits, part-time employment, and related matters under the impending condition of no compulsory retirement age. The confluence of two events—the birth of new vitality for the emeritus rank and the demise of compulsory retirement—may be fortuitous. The combination may help resolve some of the most perplexing dilemmas now being discussed.

When retirement is made desirable both by financial attractions and by benefits and privileges that are personally and academically satisfying, faculty members will decide to retire at their own volition, at any age. Alternatively, if highly valued senior faculty members are to be persuaded by administration to continue as part of the working faculty, it will be for the same reasons, namely, inducements that are personally and academically too difficult to resist. Recent studies about the emeritus rank delineate many of those attractions and inducements and illustrate how personnel procedures can utilize fresh conceptions about the meaning of emeritus status, to the mutual advantage of faculty and institution.

What Trends Presage Its Restructuring?

Several conditions that foreshadow change are evident in recent literature. The number of emeriti is large and growing. Emeriti are becoming more assertive about what they look upon as their rights. Recognition of emeriti is growing in policy statements of major professional organizations. Also, emeriti are organizing themselves and conducting conferences with themes arising from self-interest. Taken together, these conditions set the stage for a much more visible and more influential role for emeriti in higher education.

Organized emeriti groups are on record on the side of encouraging increased recognition from higher education institutions and greater participation by emeriti on campus. There are already acknowledged differences by colleges and universities in the recognition afforded retirees in general and those honored by the award of emeritus standing. The American Association of University Professors (AAUP) has recommended special prerequisites for emeriti to help maintain collegial campus contacts. Some collective bargaining agreements spell out qualifications for emeritus rank and recognize their special standing.

A sentiment prevails among responsible groups to pay attention to the fact that emeritus faculty have important contributions to make on their home campuses and elsewhere. The ongoing capability of many distinguished emeriti is readily demonstrable. For example, of the seven individuals who were the 1989 trustees of Teachers Insurance and Annuity Association/College Retirement Equities Fund (TIAA-CREF), three were university emeriti (Duke, North Carolina, Notre Dame). They held enormous responsibility as custodians and policy makers for one of the world's largest funds, an investment pool whose safeguarding is of immense importance to higher education.

Research on emeriti activities shows unequivocally that a professor who retires is no different in knowledge and skill the day after receiving the silver bowl at the retirement party from the day before. It can be predicted that any restructuring of the emeritus rank that upgrades the stature of emeriti and opens more opportunities for their participation in departmental and campus life would be welcomed.

What Changes in the Emeritus Rank Are Likely?

Essentially, the emeritus rank would become a part-time working rank for especially meritorious senior faculty, rather than solely an honorific rank reserved for those who have retired. The altered rank would carry full academic/professional standing and would provide for flexibility of conditions of employment. Transfer to that rank, with the details of responsibilities and rewards, would be negotiated on an individual basis within stated institutional policy.

How Might a New Emeritus Rank Help Solve Problems of Abolishing a Compulsory Retirement Age?

According to the literature, several problems may be exacerbated when a compulsory retirement age no longer prevails, including:

- getting rid of deadwood if there is no compulsory retirement calendar date that makes it automatic;

- keeping highly productive faculty members from taking advantage of early retirement incentives meant for others;
- continuing to pay high salaries to older professors and still find funds to hire younger ones;
- making room for younger new hires even if the funds are not available to employ them;
- containing the mounting costs of fringe benefits; and
- limiting institutional retirement fund contributions if there is no mandated ceiling.

These and other related problems will not all be solved immediately by assigning new meaning and function to the emeritus rank. It should be possible, however, to cushion the impact of some of the problems by making phased retirement more desirable for more-valued faculty members, upgrading evaluation standards and procedures to weed out unsatisfactory performers, and making early retirement more desirable for satisfactory but less productive colleagues.

What Should Colleges and Universities Do?

It would be in the institution's interest to position itself in planning about roles for emeritus professors as a partner with the present emeritus faculty body and with emeriti-soon-to-be. Some schools are already well along in such planning for the decade ahead, but many have yet to begin. The faculty senate could be the vehicle of choice in which to vest the planning function and operations, at least at first, in cooperation with the administrative planning office.

Basic data useful for planning about emeriti consist largely of information about the emeriti. Yet many institutions have little hard data bearing on the intentions and aspirations of either active faculty or emeriti. That is especially noteworthy because the emeriti themselves are generally interested in and willing to help garner and analyze such data.

Now may be the time for a significant change in the meaning, the function, and the utilization of the emeritus professor in colleges and universities. The impetus for change comes chiefly from emeriti themselves. The timeliness of the change comes from the pressing need to accommodate changes resulting from the abolition of a compulsory retirement age for tenured faculty. The proposed new meaning and functions of the emeritus rank are designed to help keep highly valued senior faculty members active on campus into their later years, to everyone's advantage and at reduced cost to the institution.

ADVISORY BOARD

CONSULTING EDITORS

Leonard L. Baird
University of Kentucky

James H. Banning
Colorado State University

Trudy W. Banta
University of Tennessee

Margaret J. Barr
Texas Christian University

Louis W. Bender
Florida State University

Rita Bornstein
University of Miami

Larry Braskamp
University of Illinois

Robert F. Carbone
University of Maryland

Jay L. Chronister
University of Virginia

Darrell Clowes
Virginia Polytechnic Institute and State University

Mary E. Dilworth
ERIC Clearinghouse on Teacher Education

James A. Eison
Southeast Missouri State University

Lawrence Erickson
Southern Illinois University

Valerie French
American University

J. Wade Gilley
George Mason University

Joseph V. Julian
Syracuse University

Jeanne M. Likens
Ohio State University

William F. Stier, Jr.
State University of New York at Brockport

REVIEW PANEL

Charles Adams
University of Amherst

Richard Alfred
University of Michigan

Philip G. Altbach
State University of New York

Louis C. Attinasi, Jr.
University of Houston

Ann E. Austin
Vanderbilt University

Robert J. Barak
State Board of Regents

Alan Bayer
Virginia Polytechnic Institute and State University

John P. Bean
Indiana University

Louis W. Bender
Florida State University

Carol Bland
University of Minnesota

Deane G. Bornheimer
New York University

John A. Centra
Syracuse University

Arthur W. Chickering
George Mason University

Jay L. Chronister
University of Virginia

Mary Jo Clark
San Juan Community College

Shirley M. Clark
University of Minnesota

Darrel A. Clowes
Virginia Polytechnic Institute and State University

CONTENTS

Foreword	**xvii**
Acknowledgments	**xix**

Introduction	**1**
Prototypes of the New Emeriti	1
The Importance of the Emeritus Professorship	2
The Meaning of "Emeritus Professor" and Related Terms	4
Tenured Faculty: A Special Group in America's Work Force	5
ADEA and Tenured Faculty	6
The Effect of a New Interpretation of the Emeritus Rank on Dilemmas in Higher Education	9
The Urgency of a New Meaning for the Emeritus Rank	13

Theory, Research, and Advocacy	**15**
The Hazards of Advocacy	15
Theories of and Research on Productive Faculty Members' Role Continuity	15
Data Available to Prepare for Uncapping	17
Additional Data Needed	20
The Realities of Aging	22
Changes Affecting the Decision to Retire	24
Evidence Suggesting Faculty Work until Later Ages	26
Current Faculty Members' Understanding of ADEA	27
The Role of Emeriti Faculty	28
Faculty Members' View of Emeritus Status	30
The Emeritus Status and Collective Bargaining	34
The Changing Role of Emeritus Faculty	34
The Relationship between Uncapping and Emeritus Status	35
Summary	36

Currents of Change	**39**
Calls for Change	39
Institutions with Compulsory Retirement	40
Institutions Awarding Emeritus Status	41
Criteria Used to Appoint Emeriti	42
Faculty Privileges	42
The Reemployment of Emeritus Faculty	43
Emeritus Faculty as Part of the "Working" Faculty	45
The Emeritus Professor Status in Collective Bargaining Contracts	46
Revising Tenure in Light of Uncapping	49
Summary	50

Findings: Policy and Practice Considerations   **53**

Timely Interpretation of the Emeritus Rank   53
The Relationship between the New Emeritus Rank
   and Existing Ranks   53
A Paradigm for Cost-Benefit Analysis   54
Future Roles for Emeriti   55
The "Portable" Emeritus Status   58
Institutional Planning for a New Emeritus Rank   58
Summary   60

Conclusions and Recommendations   **63**

Conclusions   63
Recommendations   64
Issues for Further Study   67
Summary   68

References   **69**
Index   **77**

FOREWORD

Two principal conditions in higher education are currently bringing new importance to an examination of the status of the emeritus professor: A shortage of faculty is predicted for the second half of the 1990's, and, due to growing recognition that increased age does not automatically mean decreased productivity, the practice of age-based mandatory requirement is fading.

The rank of emeritus professor is not universally accepted as a distinguished rank because it has been used for a variety of purposes. At some institutions the rank of emeritus professor is granted sparingly and based on the expectation of continued productivity. In those cases, though emeritus professors usually assume a part-time status with the institution, they are granted office space and support services, including secretarial services and travel resources. They continue to teach occasionally, act as principal investigators on research projects, chair dissertation committees, and publish journal articles and books.

At other institutions, the emeritus professor rank is used as an incentive to encourage faculty to retire and cease participating in the functions of the institution. Even *within* some institutions, confusion about the purpose of the emeritus rank leads to inconsistency in expectations among peers, supervisors and subordinates. It is no wonder that the rank of emeritus professor is not considered an incentive for continued productivity by many faculty.

In this report by James E. Mauch, professor, administrative and policy studies, and associate faculty, Center for Latin American Studies, University of Pittsburgh; Jack W. Birch, professor emeritus of psychology in education, University of Pittsburgh and Jack Matthews, emeritus professor, Cleft Palate/Craniofacial Center and Department of Communication, University of Pittsburgh, the position of emeritus professor is examined in depth. The report begins by examining the theory, research and advocacy for emeritus positions, and ends with a review of policy and practice considerations. The authors have developed the most definitive review on this rank ever published.

Several things seem to be clear. Teaching and scholarship are skills that improve when practiced over a long period of time, and the knowledge of well-seasoned professors is of great value to institutions of higher learning. Not all faculty continue to be productive in their later years, and those who do should be able to attain a respected rank. For any position or title to be held in high esteem, it must be awarded selectively and be based on consistent criteria of merit.

Higher education institutions cannot afford to miss any opportunity to maintain the most effective, intellectual and educational faculty possible. This report will be very useful for institutions which value their experienced and productive faculty and are seeking ways to keep them active within the institution beyond the normal retirement years.

Jonathan D. Fife
Series Editor
Professor of Higher Education and Director,
ERIC Clearinghouse on Higher Education
The George Washington University

ACKNOWLEDGMENTS

We wish to express our appreciation to the Alumni Research Fund of the School of Education, University of Pittsburgh, for generous support of research; to Dr. Neil Timm, director, and Rama Bazaz of the Office of Management Information and Policy Analysis, University of Pittsburgh; and to the ERIC Clearinghouse on Higher Education for valuable research help in preparation of this manuscript. And finally we would like to thank dean Tom La Belle for his support and encouragement and Ms. Yvonne Jones for her conscientious typing of the manuscript.

INTRODUCTION

This report is focused on significant developments in the emeritus rank, especially developments that promise help in solving dilemmas associated with abandonment of compulsory retirement. New Year's Day, 1994, begins an era of no compulsory retirement age for tenured higher education faculty. Current literature and preliminary reports from studies now in progress show the need for rethinking many faculty personnel policies and practices that were appropriate under the conditions of a mandatory retirement age.

. . . "emeritus professor" [may change] from a distinguished retired rank to a new form of faculty rank.

At the same time, a growing professional literature reflects activism by current and prospective emeriti, often in concert with college administrators, toward producing alternative definitions of retirement (Albert 1986; Appley 1987). For many professors, retirement no longer means withdrawal from active work at one's primary career. Instead, the option is open to continue what one has been doing, perhaps at one's own pace and under newly negotiated terms of employment.

A postulate that emerges from the literature analysis is that fast-paced higher education policy and practice changes may well alter the historical "emeritus professor" image from a distinguished retired rank to a new form of faculty rank, equally distinguished but accenting productivity, as well as individually staged progression toward full retirement. A spotlight is placed on the emeritus professor rank because it has the potential to be a salient element among all the prospective changes associated with the abandonment of a compulsory retirement age.

Prototypes of the New Emeriti

For more than 30 years, information has been accumulating that portrays the emeritus professor in an active, functioning role (Benz 1958). Emeritus faculty and their institutions, such as the following examples, and the summaries of reports and investigations that follow lend credence to the notion that a significant number of more competent senior faculty members might be willing to take formal retirement but still stay on to play important parts on campus if their institutions assured them of continuing benefits tailored to their individual needs.

Ralph S. Brown, professor emeritus of law at Yale University, is one example. Professor Brown teaches part time at another law school and has an office at Yale. He points out that if one is forced to give up an office on retirement, one's annoyance might be enough to lead to staying on as, perhaps, a not-very-enthusiastic teacher. Gordon A. Craig is a professor emeritus of history at Stanford University. Professor Craig warmly acknowledges Stanford's continued support and interest in him during 10 years of "formal" retirement. He has taught at Stanford half time during six of those 10 years, has an office on campus, has authored books, has received a Ford Foundation grant, serves on university committees for faculty and staff benefits, and maintains an otherwise active schedule (Mangan 1988).

Frederick N. Crescitelli, professor of biology at the University of California at Los Angeles, became an emeritus professor at age 70. Thinking back at age 79, he reflects that acquiring the emeritus title simply meant that he could continue, though not as an active faculty member, without a break in his work. He teaches in extension occasionally, guest lectures in regular classes, adds to his research on retinal pigmentation, and is writing a book about his investigations. Professor Crescitelli has an office and access to laboratory facilities and is eligible for many other emeriti perks simply by showing a special identification card (Blum 1988).

Beloit College Geology Professor Henry G. Woodard, at age 62, opted to be part of a four-year program that let him phase into retirement. To start, he paired with a younger colleague and shared a teaching load. That gave him increased time for research and reflection (Mangan 1988). At UCLA, Professor Thomas W. James, who took part in a phased move to emeritus status, remarks that that arrangement has two advantages. First, faculty members are given time and opportunity to make thoughtful and deliberate decisions about how to spend their later years and test some alternatives. Second, during the phasing, and perhaps longer, the university continues to have and enjoy a valued human resource, the productive senior teacher, scholar, and researcher (Blum 1988).

The Importance of the Emeritus Professorship
Emerging perceptions of the emeritus professorship include marked alterations in its meaning, its role, its function, and in criteria for attaining and maintaining the rank (Mirel 1977; Riley 1986). Testimony to these substantial changes is found in a growing body of literature, both research and philosophical. Yet there has been no published source of integrated

information on which to base generalizations about the current and future intentions or actions of faculty members who have been or might be awarded emeritus status (AAUP 1987b). Reliable, up-to-date, and representative information on those matters could be particularly useful in higher education planning now and in the immediate future. In view of these conditions, it seems important and timely to collect and analyze retirement and emeritus status data from institutional policies and practices, from the activities of faculty members, and on the current and future desires and intentions of both.

The research, philosophical, and policy and practice literature needs to be reviewed and synthesized for several reasons. One of the primary reasons is that preliminary inquiries locally and regionally reveal that although the term "emeritus" is widely used to designate the status, the meaning of "emeritus professor" varies from one institution to another. That is, the actual rights, privileges, obligations, and involvement of the emeritus professor in university affairs are inconsistent among colleges and universities. The designation of "emeritus" is contained in written policy in fewer than 50 percent of the colleges and universities surveyed (Mauch, Birch, and Matthews 1989a, 1989b).

Second, the criteria used to determine which retirees are awarded emeritus standing differ among institutions.

Third, a reason for reviewing the emeritus status now is its timeliness: Nationwide elimination of age as a criterion for retirement is scheduled to occur on January 1, 1994. The imminent elimination of any age criterion for retirement can be anticipated to exert a major influence on personnel policies and practices.

Fourth, there are already indications that the standing of tenure is being reviewed insofar as it may be impacted by the removal of a compulsory retirement age (Benjamin 1988; Ruebhausen 1989).

Fifth, whether or not uncapping of retirement age would occur, there is no doubt that intellectual and physical vigor and competence now extend, for a great many academic and professional men and women, far beyond the 65 to 70 age period established many years ago (Committee on Aging 1986; Havighurst 1985).

Taken together, these matters highlight the need for an updated view of the venerable emeritus status, including a careful examination of what forces are at work and what changes might be predicted as the countdown toward 1994 continues.

The Meaning of "Emeritus Professor" and Related Terms

The following American definition gives both meaning and derivation of the term.

> Emeritus, *plural* emeriti. *An adjective but often used as a noun . . . . So* "professor emeritus" *yields or leads to an emeritus. Specific to academics, a professor (dean, president) who upon retirement retains the title of his tenure by formal order of his college and under the same authority by which it confers degrees. (Latin* ex-, *of, out of, from:* mereri, *to merit yields or leads to* emereri, *to merit by right of service, past participle* emeritus *)* (Ciardi 1980, p. 120).

Some colleges and universities adhere to the meaning given by Ciardi and to the manner in which he states the title is awarded. For others, the definition found in the *Oxford American Dictionary* (1980 ed.) would be more applicable:

> Emeritus. *Adjective. Retired and holding an honorary title, as professor emeritus.*

The usage of "emeritus" ranges from a synonym for retired to an earned rank, conferred in the same manner as other ranks, signifying recognition for long and meritorious service to an institution of higher learning, and entitling the bearer to certain rank-connected rights and privileges. Because of the variance in usage of the term "emeritus," it will be defined, where necessary, in context.

The strict usage of "emeritus" limiting it only to academia is no longer common. In popular writing, "emeritus" is applied with rough comparability to "former" or "past," as in "emeritus board member." Extending the meaning in that fashion, some colleges and universities apply "emeritus" loosely as a synonym for "retired," with no formal authorization from a responsible institutional body. In that broad sense, it is simply a collective expression for persons who have been employed as faculty at an institution.

All members of the Association of American Universities (AAU) surveyed use the term "emeritus" to designate certain faculty; only 18 percent of AAU members use the term to designate all faculty retirees. None use other terms to mean the same as "emeritus" (Mauch, Birch, and Matthews 1989a).

The term "tenure" has a widely acknowledged meaning (AAUP 1940) (see the following section).

Other key terms are defined as follows:

- *Pension.* A periodic payment made to a person who has retired.
- *Rank, academic.* A title signifying the standing of a person employed in higher education, usually assistant, associate, or full professor, in ascending status.
- *Capped* or *capping.* The placing of an upper age limit on the duration of anything, such as employment, payments, or contract provisions.
- *Mandatory retirement age.* The provision that an employee must retire upon reaching a certain age.
- *Benefit.* A consideration other than salary provided by an employer to an employee that is viewed by the employee as having value and that is received as a condition of employment.

Tenured Faculty: A Special Group in America's Work Force

It is the widespread acknowledgment of the obligations and the privileges embodied in the academic tenure concept itself that sets tenured faculty off from most of the rest of the nation's work force. The faculty member demonstrates, during a trial employment period, the qualities the institution seeks in its full-time, permanent academic appointees. The faculty member is then awarded a tenured post, which guarantees continued employment until retirement so long as work performance remains satisfactory and prevailing moral/ethical standards are not abridged. Promotions, work-performance evaluations, and similar matters are based on established criteria that maximize collegiality and objectivity in decision making. In effect, the faculty and the institution make promises to each other that have the force of binding contracts that, once made, may not be summarily or arbitrarily broken (AAUP 1940).

Tenure is said to have begun in the Middle Ages as another form of protection altogether, namely to safeguard medieval professors from physical violence because of embracing and teaching unpopular ideas or beliefs (Hellweg and Churchman 1981). Freedom to present out-of-favor concepts still needs protection on today's campuses. But tenure now goes farther, affording security against dismissal other than for defined causes and situations that can be examined in a court of law. Because of the job protection tenure provides, it is sometimes criticized as a virtual guarantee of a life sinecure (Ruebhausen 1989; Ruebhausen and Woodruff 1986).

It is the "unending" attribute of academic tenure that causes concern about the abandonment of compulsory retirement. The arrival at compulsory retirement age now puts a decisive end to permanent tenure. But without a compulsory retirement age, the tenure contract has no "natural" termination point. While other groups may have similar tenure arrangements, higher education faculty have been singled out and exempted from the provisions of the Age Discrimination in Employment Act (ADEA) (Ruebhausen 1989).

ADEA and Tenured Faculty

The Employment Act of 1946 was the earliest identifiable effort of the U.S. Congress and the administrative branch to legislate an end to arbitrary upper age limits on employment. The Older Americans Act of 1965 was a second attempt in the same direction. Neither the 1946 nor the 1965 act had the necessary enforcement provisions to accomplish their intent.

The Age Discrimination in Employment Act was enacted on December 15, 1967, as P.L. 90–202 and became effective June 12, 1968. The purposes of the act, quoting from the statute, are:

> . . . to promote employment of older persons based on their ability rather than age; to prohibit arbitrary age discrimination in employment; to help employers and workers find ways of meeting problems arising from the impact of age on employment.

Specifically, the ADEA attempted to provide for the nation a firm, enforceable requirement that no one up to the age of 65 would be presumed incompetent solely by reason of age (Committee on Aging 1986).

In debate on the act, Congress weighed two sides of the matter of age discrimination in employment. One side was the free and unimpeded exercise by businesses and other agencies of managerial decision making and control. The other side was the interests of older workers who might be unjustly limited in their attempts to obtain or continue in employment by policies based on incorrect assumptions about the effect of age on ability. The result of the debate was a congressional decision to attempt, through legislation, to be fair both to employers and to employees by preventing *arbitrary* policies that could unjustifiably prevent persons over a specific age from being employed as their abilities warranted. Rep. Burke noted during the debate that "discrimination arises because of assumptions that are made about the effects of age on performance. As a general rule, ability is age-less" (Committee on Aging 1986).

As originally passed, the ADEA protected persons up to age 65, but it did not cover federal, state, or local government employees. Therefore, state colleges and universities were exempt from the law's provisions; however, private institutions were subject to the ADEA. The enactment of P.L. 93–257 in 1974, the Fair Labor Standards Act Amendments, broadened the coverage of the ADEA to most government employees, excepting elected officials, foreign service officers, Central Intelligence Agency employees, and air traffic controllers. Also excepted were law enforcement officers, fire fighters, and pilots or first officers on commercial flights (Prochaska 1987).

In 1978, the ADEA was amended to increase the upper age limit protected against discrimination through age 69 but stopped upon attainment of age 70. The amendment stated "at least 40 years of age but less than 70 years of age."

In 1982, with the passage of P.L. 97 248, the ADEA protected group health plans, requiring that employees and their spouses aged 65 or older be supplied the same group health coverage under the same conditions as employees and spouses under age 65. That prevents employers from shifting persons to Medicare as the primary payer at an arbitrary age (Prochaska 1987).

The ADEA of 1986 bans discrimination on the basis of age, not only with respect to continuation of employment but also with respect to recruitment, opportunities for employment, compensation, terms, conditions, or privileges of employment, and retirement benefits. The ADEA has also been extended to include all persons in the civilian labor force who are at least 40 years of age. Where state law is stronger in prohibiting age discrimination, it takes precedence. For example, many states have eliminated mandatory retirement ages for employees, including tenured professors (Committee on Aging 1986).

A number of exceptions or exemptions appeared in the 1978 amendments and remained in the 1986 amendments. The following hold special relevance for higher education:

1. Compulsory retirement may be required of "any employee who has attained 65 years of age and who . . . is employed in a bona fide executive or a high policy-making position, if such employee is entitled to an immediate non-forfeitable annual retirement benefit [that] equals, in the aggregate, at least $44,000."
2. Effective with P.L. 99–592, paragraph 6, the ADEA permits, until December 31, 1993, compulsory retirement for any employee 70 years old who is serving under a contract of unlimited tenure. The 1986 amendments call for a study regarding the likely consequences of eliminating mandatory retirement on higher education institutions (Committee on Aging 1986).

The first of the above exemptions is open to several questions of interpretation as to employment in higher education. For example, what title defines "a bona fide executive or a high policy-making position" in a college or university? Dean? Provost? Department head? Or will the determination rest on the contents of a job description? Also, in some decisions about collective bargaining, the professoriat has, as a body, been classed as managers. Does that qualify them for the first exemption?

The two exemptions are in force at present. Experienced congressional observers predict that the second exemption will be eliminated and that the first will at least be modified by hiking the income figure. It is the elimination of the second exemption—the elimination of mandatory retirement—that can make higher education's current dilemmas even more perplexing.

The Effect of a New Interpretation of the Emeritus Rank on Dilemmas in Higher Education

• *How can early retirement incentives be installed that do not denude the institution of its most valued faculty in their best years?*

A high priority topic in the 1970s and 1980s was ways and means of encouraging early retirement. According to Kellams and Chronister (1988), the proffered incentives worked: Faculty were motivated to retire early. However, their study found that both the more and the less productive faculty took advantage of the opportunity to leave early. Their reasons were different, but the institutions were left with a "good news–bad news" result.

There are several distinctly different points of view about what faculty members want for themselves in their later years. True enough, there are many things on which the great majority of older faculty members seem to agree. They desire financial security, health insurance, continued relationships with their institutions and colleagues, a sense of usefulness and of being needed and appreciated, and the opportunity to pursue their own interests (Auerbach 1986a, 1986c; Dorfman 1985). It is on the latter two of the above desires, though, that sharply different points of view may be emerging.

To illustrate the various viewpoints, one can use extreme positions about what faculty members mean when they talk about being useful, needed, and appreciated and finding the opportunity to pursue their own interests.

For one segment of faculty, those desires may be very well satisfied by tutoring the occasional undergraduate or graduate student, by having a place in the department area to receive mail, to use the Faculty Club and the library, to have occasional use of an office, to make and receive phone calls, and to have an account at the book store.

Some faculty members, of course, are content—perhaps even pleased—simply to walk out on the day of retirement, never to return. That is probably a small minority, however. Other retiring faculty members, for health or other reasons, move almost immediately to places distant from the campuses where they had their careers. Still others, while remaining in the university neighborhood, become caught up in a second career or recreational activities that leave them little time or inclination for more than casual interest in their former activities and associates. It is not clear how many fall in these three "little or no involvement" groups. It may be a substantial number or a small one (Benz 1958; Holden 1985; Sumberg 1989).

But many, perhaps a large number of, faculty members (Albert 1986; Dorfman 1982, 1984, 1985) may want something in retirement much different from what has just been described. They may really want simply to continue to do essentially what they have been doing but to move to a somewhat slower beat of the drum (Trice 1981). The question remains: What should higher education institutions offer as early retirement policies that will be both sensible about the realities of institutional resources and sensitive to the personal, academic, and professional capabilities and aspirations of faculty members in the late years of their productive lives?

Highly productive faculty do accept early retirement options that are too attractive to pass up (Kellams and Chronister 1988). But the highly productive early leavers also say that retirement is attractive to them because they want to continue in their academic and professional work, though perhaps in more limited, more focused, or more flexible ways (Kellams and Chronister 1988; Rowe 1976). Benefits that will hold productive faculty can be individually designed and offered under the control of the institution if proper policies are developed regarding them and if the practices that flow from the policies can accommodate many different sets of faculty requirements and wishes.

Making the emeritus professorship a working rank and building into that rank the flexibility sought by highly productive individuals could help resolve the dilemma of how to have a desirable retirement program and still keep highly productive professors from leaving. The details of such an arrangement are suggested in the next section.

• *How can institutions reconcile the high cost of keeping productive senior faculty longer and the need to invest more in promising beginners?*

That dilemma cannot be resolved if institutions are required to operate on only present funding plus cost-of-living adjustments as the income side of their salary budgets. Money for new hires would certainly be scarce in that case. And with the prospect of even a few years' increase in average retirement age—something that would certainly be possible with no compulsory retirement age (Lozier and Dooris 1988–89)—salary budgets would have to surge to meet the increased costs at the highest levels. The most determined efforts for increased public and private support would be unlikely to produce sufficient income each year to stay abreast of increased requirements, much less go beyond them.

Not only may colleges and universities be called upon to find ways to pay higher salaries for a longer time; the initial cost of new hires may also rise during the same time. To reveal why that may occur it is first necessary to look back a few years.

A major element in Congress's rationale for previously exempting tenured faculty in the ADEA was the fear that removing a mandatory retirement age for professors would, for years, restrict the employment of new faculty. Higher education associations lobbied for, endorsed, and supported Congress's position at that time. Analysis of recent data (Lozier and Dooris 1987) from AAU members now suggests that Congress may have been misled in exempting professors from the ADEA uncapping in the first place. Rather than being able to select from a glut of candidates, it appears likely to be difficult in the decade ahead for colleges and universities to find qualified replacement faculty (Bowen and Sosa 1989).

One response to a dearth of young prospects is to reduce the need for them. That calls for policies that would decelerate retirement to a degree containing the need for new faculty at its source. The solution to financial support is related. One thing most potential retirees are concerned about is the prospect of facing rising inflation with fixed income. Therefore, faculty nearing retirement are likely to be amenable to negotiated arrangements that minimize that possibility.

If the emeritus status became a working rank that embodied opportunities for reduced load and assured continuity of employment, that could help resolve the issue of how to keep productive senior faculty longer while sharply cutting the cost of doing so. At the same time, if the need for new faculty abated, the funds released through reduced senior faculty loads would be available for new hires.

... criteria other than age may need to be applied to bring an end to tenure for a faculty member.

- *How can teaching, research, and service standards for faculty be implemented so as to minimize the accumulation of "deadwood" under conditions of unlimited tenure without compulsory retirement?*

Almost every societal unit, including higher education, has some deadwood in it. The tenured faculty members so characterized tend to be indifferent teachers, low in research or other scholarly activity, and disengaged from service in their departments or their professional and academic societies.

As long as tenure stopped at a specific age (now 70), age offered some surcease to faculty colleagues or administrators from tenure award mistakes or reduced competence of professors. With uncapping, however, it is possible that tenure may be an award for life. It may not be feasible to wait out a problem tenured appointment and let the calendar solve it. Instead, criteria other than age may need to be applied to bring an end to tenure for a faculty member (Licata 1986).

It is held by both administration and faculty, for much the same reasons, that the most difficult decisions in higher education today are those concerning the award of tenure (Miller 1987). The level of stress already present in tenure determinations will almost certainly heighten with the U.S. Supreme Court's unanimous decision on January 9, 1990, that the Equal Employment Opportunity Commission may examine confidential papers that universities relied upon in tenure disputes. The difficulty of such decisions can only increase further in the foreseeable future, when uncapping becomes the rule.

The prospect of uncapping is already placing heavier responsibility on the promotion and tenure awarding structure and mechanisms of colleges and universities. From the faculty side in particular there is movement toward evaluation by objectives and toward specification of promotion and tenure award criteria rather than dependence upon abstractly worded principles imbedded in unwritten institutional lore (Miller 1987). From all sides there are calls for the will to make hard decisions in "gray" areas, for rigorous quality control, and for high-status faculty members to be given ample time to serve on promotion and tenure committees.

Early retirement incentives can be depended upon to motivate many "low productive" faculty members to leave (Kellams and Chronister 1988). Two problems remain: to motivate younger "low productive" faculty members to mend their ways and to prevent potential "low productives" from obtaining tenure.

There could be special roles for emeritus professors in the management of both those problems. Older faculty members ". . . may frequently mislay their glasses, but that does not impair the wisdom and judgment that other societies have venerated in their elders" (Brown 1988, p. 35). One decision point where both richness of wisdom and unusually sound judgments are of particular value to the institution is at the initial employment of faculty. Others are when tenure or promotion are being considered. Emeritus professors could contribute strongly as consultants, committee members, and committee chairs.

Such responsibilities and roles for emeriti may be derogated by some who believe that older faculty have lost touch with the cutting edges of their professions and academic disciplines. Our literature searches, however, turned up neither research evidence nor well-documented experiences to indicate that senior professors were any less in contact than younger faculty with current and recent developments in their fields. As to the motivation by senior faculty of young tenured laggards, there is a substantial amount of anecdotal evidence that deliberate mentorship by emeriti can generate positive changes (Mauch, Birch, and Matthews 1989a).

The Urgency of a New Meaning for the Emeritus Rank
Serious proposals have already been published in an effort to establish, in operational terms, what rights and responsibilities should inhere in the emeritus status (Albert 1986). Faculty members with emeritus rank, vigorously active and alert in personal, professional, and scholarly matters, are making their voices heard in new and constructive ways, to the benefit of the academic community as a whole (Auerbach 1986a, 1986b, 1986c; Peterson, Small, and Schneider n.d.; Riley 1986). For many professors, retirement no longer means withdrawal from active work at their primary career. Instead, the option is open to continue what they have been doing, in various respects, at their own pace and under newly negotiated terms with their institutions. It is time to begin a broader review of this potential redefinition of faculty retirement.

Second, faculty members nationally are in the early stages of awareness about age uncapping and its implications for their retirement planning. The impact of uncapping promises to be a growing topic of interest to tenured faculty members who face a future without a mandatory age requirement. Finances and feelings are involved, too. "Views about the relative advantages of work and leisure and various combinations thereof may change as a person ages. The views of one's future preference between work and leisure held at age 60 are likely to be quite different from what they turn out to be at age 65 or 70" (Soldofsky 1986, p. 23).

Third, the emerging changes in the role and function of the emeritus professor may well presage a major modification in the conventional professorial rank structure in higher education (Albert 1986).

Fourth, and finally, there is a growing concern about how to maintain the positive elements in both the tenure system and the present operating retirement schemes while accommodating a new (and potentially disruptive) condition, namely, the elimination of any mandatory retirement age (Finkin 1989). Higher education groups of almost all kinds and persuasions are preoccupied with one or another facet of that problem (Heller 1986; Holden and Hansen 1989c).

This literature review and analysis should make explicit the interactions among the above four matters. Also, the review results in recommendations for actions by responsible agencies and groups and points to areas for further investigation.

THEORY, RESEARCH, AND ADVOCACY

The Hazards of Advocacy

Many groups pursue their own agendas as they address the current and future role of tenure, the aging professoriat, the promise of uncapping, the recent assertive thinking about emeritus status, collective bargaining, or the future of faculty recruitment. The points of view espoused, for example, by associations of universities and by associations of faculty members overlap, but they certainly are not identical. Moreover, each group can be expected to attend most closely to studies that seem to vindicate or support the main thrusts of their own viewpoints.

Advocates sometimes apply pressure, more or less subtly. Also, skillful advocates attempt to apply what the press calls "spin"; that is, they state a matter in a way calculated to put their own actions in a favorable light.

Advocacy certainly has a legitimate role in academe as well as in the broader society. However, advocacy is out of place—even hazardous—if it biases a literature review such as this one. Aware of that, we have tried to avoid arguing or pleading any special interest's case. Instead, our objective has been to search out and report relevant information even-handedly.

Theories of and Research on Productive Faculty Members' Role Continuity

Is there reason to think that a large proportion of successful professors really desire to keep on doing, in retirement, what they did as full-time faculty members? Or do most of them welcome the "freedom" of retirement as an earned reward that cuts them loose from the pressures and constraints of work?

A psychological and sociological theory of disengagement in aging that seems particularly relevant to the above questions was proposed 30 years ago by Cummings et al. (1960). That theory was invoked by Rose (1965) in tracking and analyzing changes with age in the activities of scientists. One key point in the theory proposes that, as the individual ages, separation widens between that person and any societal system (e.g., a college or university) of which the person has been a part, and that the drawing apart is mutual (and perhaps normal and natural). Both Rose (1965) and later Roman and Taietz (1967) are critical of the theory for its reliance on presumed states of readiness for disengagement on the parts of both the individual and the social institution involved. They

propose that "state of readiness," a vague and ill-defined entity, be replaced by more tangible "opportunity structures," which refer to whether the parties (individual and institution) put forward to each other actual evidences of a desire to be either disengaged or more closely engaged. Examples in the present case would be benefits contingent upon either termination or continued employment and benefits that would exercise either negative or positive valence, either discouraging or encouraging disengagement.

While rigorous empirical investigations of role continuity intentions or behavior among older faculty are few in number, the limited evidence in the literature weighs heavily in favor of a continuing desire for engagement and for role continuity among emeriti faculty. Moreover, there is some evidence of the same where colleges and universities are concerned.

Roman and Taietz (1967) wrote of emeritus standing as not merely honorific, a status without a role, but instead a functioning, performing position with job continuity in a flexible position whose nature is a blend of the individual's preretirement activities and postretirement interests. At their school (Cornell), some preretirement activities, such as research, permitted almost direct transfer into emeritus activities. If significant alterations in role proved necessary, as when teaching or administrative functions were taken on by new persons, the changes in role were facilitated by formal and informal user-friendly procedures within the institution.

Beginning in 1964, Roman and Taietz studied the postretirement activities of 74 professors emeriti. Thirty remained engaged with their own universities and nine with other universities. Eighteen could not work because of health reasons. Seventeen were disengaged both from their university and from their prior professions. Thus, 70 percent of those who were physically able to maintain engagement did so as professors emeriti.

The investigation on role continuity into retirement at universities by Roman and Taietz (1967), the related study by Benz (1958) with New York University faculty, the work of Roe (1965) with eminent research scientists, and the report on the wishes of emeriti by Albert (1986) all point to the high importance of structured opportunities that are visible and inviting in the determination of continued engagement between the emeritus faculty member and the higher education institution. Though disengagement may be a mutually satisfying adaptation to retirement for the American work force in general, that is evidently not necessarily true in the case of productive senior faculty members and their colleges and universities.

Another set of theoretical constructs of potential value in understanding and predicting the interactive behavior of older scholars and their institutions has its roots in cultural anthropology (Cronk 1989). This theory, though not so precisely stated as that of Cummings et al. (1960), argues the point that the acceptance of benefits carries obligations, including both reciprocity and gratitude. The productive academician has, over time, made contributions to the institution. (It is common to speak of a faculty member's "contributions," for example.) The university or college provides support and benefits, tempered by the nature and quality of the work of the faculty member. There is presumed to be gratitude on both sides.

Though "giving" may appear intrinsically benevolent, the act, according to this theory, also contains some degree of power to govern, to mollify, to embarrass, to antagonize— in short, to serve more selfish ends. Though Cronk's notions are imaginative and stimulating, no empirical research on the emeritus status or on retirement was found that utilized such cultural anthropological theorizing.

In sum, there are at least two theoretical approaches that can be taken in attempting to understand the relations between emeriti and their institutions. Though limited, the empirical studies point to structured opportunities as a very important element in facilitating continued engagement between emeriti and higher education institutions.

Data Available to Prepare for Uncapping
Information on the actual age of retirement in the past would be an important guide. If actual age of retirement is not associated with the mandatory retirement age, then the advent of uncapping may be less threatening.

Most of the literature deals with the retirement behavior of the general population, but there is a small body of research on retirement behavior of employees of higher education and an even smaller body that deals with retirement behavior of tenured faculty in higher education. There are differences reported in research on the three groups.

In the general population, there is evidence from the U.S. Department of Labor (DOL) that participation by men aged

65 and over has been declining in the general labor force since before the turn of the century. In 1890, 71 percent of men 65 and over participated in the labor force; by 1980, it was 18 percent and declining. Even in men 55 to 64, who have traditionally participated heavily in the labor force, the rate dropped from 83 percent in 1970 to 71 percent in 1981. The participation of women 65 and over has also declined, but age groups of women under 65 have increased their share of labor market participation (U.S. Department of Labor 1982).

Data from the Social Security Administration suggest a pattern of earlier ages of retirement. The percentage of individuals starting their benefits at 62 increased from 41 percent in 1967 to 58 percent in 1980, while those who began benefits at 65 and older dropped from 38 percent in 1967 to 19 percent in 1980 (Ycas 1987). Thus, if beginning to take social security benefits means stopping work, substantial numbers of older workers have been leaving the general labor force.

Yet data as to older persons' interests indicate that the majority of currently retired persons and those approaching retirement would be interested in part-time employment. More than half of all persons 65 and over now working are employed part time (U.S. Department of Labor 1982). These data may have implications for faculty as well.

With respect to higher education, studies were done in the early 1980s by the DOL (1982) at the time when the mandatory retirement age was changed from 65 to 70. The 1978 amendments to the ADEA included a provision for delaying until 1982 the change in mandatory retirement age for tenured faculty to enable institutions of higher education to make appropriate plans for the advent of the age 70 cap. The DOL study found that predicting faculty retirement age choices was more difficult than doing so for the general population because of tenure, emeritus status, better health status, and differing expectations for continued productivity.

Nevertheless, the DOL findings indicated that in 1980, 52 percent of the institutions (employing 68 percent of all faculty) already had a policy of retirement age 70 or above, while 20 percent (employing 12 percent of faculty) had no retirement age cap whatsoever. The study predicted that raising the age to 70 would result in an upward shift in the age distribution, somewhat higher costs, and declines in hiring rates but that they would be followed by a smooth adjustment to the new policy. While the estimates were based on an assumption of a moderate increase in faculty members choosing to retire after age 65, such an increase had not, in fact, taken place at institutions that voluntarily shifted retirement age from 65 to 70 (U.S. Department of Labor 1982).

Based on her own research, as well as others', Holden (1985) found that faculty in higher education retire at a much later age than the general population, they do not appear to be anxious to retire, and they wish to remain active even after retirement. Faculty see their professional career as a lifetime commitment, not one that can be brought to an end at the convenience of the institution.

Yet other studies have reported varying results on faculty retirement age. In examining a subgroup of the AAU institutions, Dooris and Lozier (1987) found that average age of retirement had actually gone down slightly over five academic years in the early 1980s, from 65.5 in 1981–82 to 64.8 in 1985–86. This time span covered the years when the federally mandated retirement age for tenured faculty rose from 65 to 70 and many institutions had early retirement programs.

Committee A on Academic Freedom and Tenure of the AAUP reported the results of a review of available information on the consequences of "uncapping" in states where it had already occurred. For all practical purposes, Committee A concluded that nothing useful had been learned from that set of inquiries because of small samples and erratic reporting (AAUP 1987b).

In 1987, the Consortium on Financing Higher Education (COFHE) studied 36 selected institutions and found that the average age of retirement rose from 64.6 in academic year 1982, to 65.2 in 1983 and 1984, to 65.3 in 1985, and to 66 in 1986. In the study population, 72 percent of faculty retired at an age earlier than the mandatory retirement age (COFHE 1989).

A similar study was conducted by TIAA-CREF in 1988 (Gray 1989). The TIAA-CREF study was based on data collected from more than 1,300 faculty and nonfaculty employees between the ages of 55 and 70 at institutions that participate in TIAA-CREF. Of the respondents who had specific retirement plans, 32 percent planned to retire before turning 65, 21 percent at age 65, 24 percent between the ages of 65 and 69, and 21 percent at age 70 or after.

Tenured faculty members, who accounted for 37 percent of the respondents, were more likely than other employees to project later retirement ages. Among tenured faculty who had specific plans, 23 percent planned to retire before age 65, 22 percent at age 65, 24 percent between the ages of 65 and 69, and 28 percent at age 70 or later. Even more interesting, among faculty who had no fixed plans but who estimated likely retirement ages, only 5 percent felt they might retire before age 65, 17 percent at age 65, 25 percent between the ages of 65 and 69, and 53 percent at age 70 or later.

Thus, based on conflicting research results, it seems that the decision to retire is complex indeed and that legally mandated age of retirement is only one factor. Other factors might include the health and vigor of the individual, the family situation, the attractiveness of the work and workplace, the financial aspects of the decision, and the desire to continue a productive professional life after retirement.

There seem to be no clear trends with respect to how long—or to what age—faculty can be expected to work. Nor do the data support patterns by type of faculty. Therefore, uncapping may not have much of an influence statistically. However, it takes some time for people to adjust to new realities, and faculty attitudes may change. The most recent study of anticipated retirement age among tenured faculty who are TIAA-CREF participants (Gray 1989) found some evidence that tenured faculty are beginning to project later retirement ages in recent years. After all, the chance to continue after age 70 is a relatively new possibility and even now is not open to many faculty who will reach age 70 prior to 1994.

Additional Data Needed

Because colleges and universities have highly educated and specialized work forces, it is often difficult or impossible to replace retiring personnel at the same level. Also, it is difficult to reassign surplus faculty who have a right to stay on.

Faculty are also mobile, and universities often find themselves in competitive situations. It is by no means clear that there will be enough qualified faculty in certain academic disciplines or professional areas to supply higher education in the future. Some evidence from the United States as well as abroad indicates that the future supply of higher education faculty may be sparse, not abundant (Bowen and Schuster 1986; Bowen and Sosa 1989). If this projection is true, good data and planning may help to assure a steady and appropriate supply of high-quality faculty.

Lozier and Dooris (1988–89) summarized the limited information on forecasting academic staff requirements by predicting two challenges directly ahead. One challenge is to find able replacements for the many faculty who will retire by the year 2000. Among their suggestions for coping with that major problem are the monitoring of "faculty flow" in more detail and changing the stereotypes about appropriate or "normal" retirement age.

The encouragement of transfer to emeritus professor rank could certainly be part of the solution to the faculty replacement problem highlighted by Lozier and Dooris. Greater individualization of faculty flow monitoring could more precisely identify incipient vacancies and could lessen the urgency of finding acceptable new hires if hard-to-replace faculty would phase into full retirement over a longer period of time as working emeritus professors.

The importance of policies that encourage the selective retention of high-performing faculty is emphasized by Lee (1989). Information should be garnered on which faculty members might be especially targeted for inducements to stay simply because of their outstanding work or, additionally, because they are qualified in fields where shortages can be predicted. Lee recommends systematically banking information for the institution's use, including information on faculty ages, supply trends in teaching and research fields, and surveys of faculty that reveal what benefits they particularly prize or would like to earn. Open participation of the faculty seems very desirable, too, in designing incentives to stay.

The second major challenge, according to Lozier and Dooris (1988–89), is the dismissal of faculty members with excellent early records who wish to continue to teach despite unacceptably lessened competency and ability to perform. It may be possible to help entice those deserving but no longer fit faculty members into retirement by assuring them a package of postretirement continuing benefits and relationships that does not include continued employment. How best to do that, and how to develop and implement a broadly acceptable evaluation system to appraise competence and ability, are topics for another report (Miller 1987).

Institutions could analyze more of their own institutional information in anticipation of uncapping, as well as keep up with new studies being done nationally. Within each institution, it may be time to study both the past retirement behav-

It is by no means clear that there will be enough qualified faculty . . . to supply higher education in the future.

ior and the future retirement intentions of faculty by categories, such as age, sex, race, academic discipline, and academic
preparation (Lee 1989).

Institutions could also study the supply and demand for
faculty by discipline or professional area, as well as projected
student demand. These factors, along with past behavior and
present intentions about faculty retirement, might guide policy
with respect to early retirement programs, as well as programs
to retain outstanding older faculty in some capacity. In addition, in an era without a forced retirement age, higher education institutions that provide unlimited tenure might be
wise to study ways to assess fairly and accurately faculty performance, an area of benign neglect presently in many universities (Miller 1987). Such studies would seem prudent in
each institution as a preparation for uncapping and as a way
to inform and involve faculty in studies relevant to their
futures.

The Realities of Aging

Reports about elderly people occupy increasing proportions
of both radio and television time and of all forms of periodical
print material. Popular publications and scholarly writing
about senior citizens absorb more and more of the time of
creative persons. Local, state, national, and international political leaders are seeking support from senior citizen constit-
uencies and are developing legislation to address the social
consequences of the steadily extending human life span. Public concern is high, and the body of knowledge about aging
multiplies.

Summarized in the following paragraphs are several key
concepts about aging culled from existing literature. These
concepts about aging are of central importance when con-
sidering emerging roles for emeritus faculty. We call these
concepts *realities* because they seem to be both basic and
highly relevant. They must be faced by those leaders among
faculty and administration who are responsible for searching
out accommodations that are both honorable and pragmatic
ways to adjust policies and practices to imminent changes
in the emeritus professor population.

Reality #1: Life span and economic implications

Americans are living longer. Persons reaching age 65 in 1989
had an average life expectancy of 20 years. Four years earlier,

in 1985, the life expectancy of a 65-year-old was 17 years. Thus, it is plain that faculty members need to plan for increasing life expectancies and for the heightened likelihood that, when retired, they will need self-support funds for a longer period of time plus provision for escalating living costs (Committee on Aging 1986; Pifer and Bronte 1986; Ycas 1987). Moreover, they could well become members of four- or five-generation families. Older faculty members may have to care, socially and economically, for their own aging parents while also giving financial assistance to younger kin, in increasing degrees. At present, for example, elderly people are four times as likely to give financial aid to their offspring as they are to receive it from them. One obvious possible solution for professors is to extend the years of earning prior to full retirement.

Reality #2: Health and intellect
Today's 70-year-olds are substantially more healthy and intellectually active than those of previous generations. People attain their 60s, 70s, and 80s in better general condition than did previous generations. Also, health and productivity are positively connected. Hence, it is imperative that higher education planners upgrade realistically their conceptions of "typical" persons in the sixth, seventh, and later decades of life rather than maintain stereotypes based on their observations of retirees of decades past or even of current retirees. Physical and mental vigor remain for adults into advanced years, and the upper limits have not yet been ascertained (Committee on Aging 1986; Ycas 1987).

Reality #3: Growing numbers
According to the Committee on Aging (1986), the U.S. population over age 65 has been increasing at more than twice the rate for persons under 65 (2.5 percent per year versus 1 percent per year). Such a differential rate of increase suggests that the number of faculty members eligible to enter the emeritus ranks may be outgrowing annually the number of scholars and professionals eligible for initial employment as faculty members. Certainly there will be variance in growth among the many academic and professional disciplines. However, the overall picture appears to be one that threatens to lead to faculty shortages if present retirement practices continue. And any institutional expansion would appear likely to aggravate the condition.

Reality #4: Differences among older persons

Those who are highly educated are more likely to continue to engage in intellectual pursuits and will experience substantial increases in intellect over a lifetime. For example, a 1989 college graduate will possess about 50 percent of the vocabulary he or she will have acquired by age 65 (approximately 22,000 versus 45,000 words).

Recent gerontological thinking tends to assign those over 65 into three groups (though there is much overlap):

- People aged 65 to 74 are generally active and healthy, usually well able to carry on the managerial, intellectual, and creative activities they engaged in before 65. A number become even more productive during those years.
- Individuals from 75 to 84 differ from the first group chiefly in pace of activities, with little or no loss of skills or intellectual vigor. Many have lost spouses and have adopted a more moderate lifestyle out of choice, not necessity.
- The over-85 group, increasing in numbers, is less well understood. It does appear that approximately half of them continue in very much the same lifestyle as the 75 to 84 age cohort. The remainder seem to move more and more into what has been called a "retired life pattern," with some level of care provided by others in areas of personal and home management. That contrasts with fewer than 15 percent of individuals aged 65 to 74 needing such support (Committee on Aging 1986; Pifer and Bronte 1986).

The above "stages of aging" described by gerontologists and the evidence about older persons' intellectual integrity and continued development dispute the notion of general debility and loss of competence with increasing age. From all indications, older persons are, as a class, becoming smarter, healthier, and more productive. Elderly people today are more competent than their counterparts of past generations.

Changes Affecting the Decision to Retire

Several ingredients other than those associated directly with extended life span may very well motivate faculty members to continue to work as long as possible. Other factors that seem to encourage putting off retirement appear to be rooted in tax policies, benefits, and political or economic considerations (Sumberg 1989). Four major elements are based on Sumberg's analysis:

1. The age at which unreduced social security benefits will be paid has been increased, thus encouraging potential retirees to defer retirement until they can receive full benefits. That age is scheduled to increase again in the year 2000. It will move steadily up to age 66 for those who reach age 62 in the year 2005 and will reach age 67 for those who turn age 62 in 2022. At the same time, benefits paid to early retirees at age 62 will be reduced by 30 percent rather than by the current rate of 20 percent. Moreover, motivation for putting off applying for social security at the current age for full benefits (age 65) should be heightened due to the scheduled rise in the deferred retirement credit from 3 percent to 8 percent per year between 1995 and 2013. The fact that social security benefits have become taxable for earners in the income range common for faculty members may well be an added deterrent to taking the payments any earlier than necessary.
2. Employer-paid medical benefits may no longer be reduced at the employer's discretion at age 65. For most of America's employees, employer-based health insurance coverage cannot be terminated because of age; that is, it must be extended to employees over 70 years of age. Unless the current law is changed, faculty members could continue to participate in employer-sponsored health insurance programs past age 70.
3. Current legislation (ADEA) prohibits employers from ceasing contributions at any specific age to pension plans of tenured faculty. Unless there are changes in legislation or institutional plans, as of January 1, 1994, tenured faculty members will also be eligible to continue to build pension benefits, without regard to age. Thus, there is no longer an age-specific trigger in the pension acquisition process to suggest a time schedule for retirement.
4. For almost two decades, the higher education community has sought ways to increase desirable early retirement options for faculty. The 1986 Tax Reform Act (TRA) impeded those efforts in several ways. Perhaps most evident was the strict limit placed on the employment of

salary-reduction savings plans, lump-sum payments, and the use of other tax-deferred arrangements as incentives for faculty members to retire early. It promises to be some time before the TRA regulations become sufficiently clarified for new financial accommodations attractive to faculty members to emerge.

After careful consideration of factors such as the four briefly noted above, Sumberg concluded that they would probably have little influence on the timing of retirement for faculty members prior to 1990. But, he added:

Perhaps as social security and tax rules discourage early retirement and allow employees to continue working, to retain their health insurance, and to accrue pension benefits beyond age 70, attitudes toward retirement among a new generation of faculty members will change. Such new attitudes could lead even more faculty members to continue teaching and research beyond age 70 (Sumberg 1989, p. 13).

Even a modest move in the direction suggested by Sumberg could have a major impact on the financing and on the faculty structure of higher education.

Evidence Suggesting Faculty Work until Later Ages

The ages at which faculty retire, important information for planning purposes, may well vary with the type of institution, with the nature of the options available to faculty employed at those institutions, and with how well faculty are treated by the institutions. For example, a common assumption is that faculty at AAU institutions who teach a few graduate students and concentrate on research may find retirement less appealing than faculty at community colleges who teach a large number of classes and students on a rather rigid schedule (Blum 1989a). But there is little evidence to support or reject that assumption.

Further, options at retirement for individual faculty vary greatly. On one hand, there are faculty who are so well provided for at retirement that the decision to retire is not an economic one; at the other extreme are those faculty who face lost fringe benefits and substantial income loss upon retirement. Finally, there are those institutions where morale and conditions of employment are so fine that faculty regret leaving and do not look forward to the day they have to retire; conversely, there are institutions where faculty can hardly contain their enthusiasm at the prospect of leaving.

Some very recent evidence suggests that faculty may now intend to work to later ages. The study surveying TIAA-CREF participants' expected age of retirement (Gray 1989) supports this theory. This study also reviewed some results of an earlier, similar study done in 1979. When the expected retirement ages of TIAA-CREF participants in 1988 were compared with those in 1979, there were some surprises. Proportionately fewer of those in the 1988 study (22 percent) gave an expected retirement age of 65 than in the 1979 group (37 percent), while a larger proportion (22 percent) listed age 70 than in the earlier study (15 percent). Higher percentages of respondents in 1988 also gave an expected retirement age between 66 and 69 (31 percent versus 19 percent) and under 65 (18 percent versus 16 percent).

Many in both studies were not tenured faculty. When the TIAA-CREF participant data from 1988 were reworked to examine tenured faculty only, it was evident that tenured faculty in the 1988 study planned to retire at later ages than did other annuitants.*

Current Faculty Members' Understanding of ADEA
Faculty seem to have little understanding of the effects of uncapping. Perhaps they are too engrossed in their work, or it may be that the idea of retirement seems so far in the future that it is out of sight, out of mind. The authors conducted a small, informal survey of colleagues, and that survey reinforced the impression described above.

However, information is increasingly available to faculty through publications like the *Chronicle of Higher Education*, *Academe*, and conferences or workshops, such as those put on by the American Council on Education, AAUP, the American Federation of Teachers (AFT), COFHE, and the National Education Association (NEA). Faculty may also seem to be unimpressed or uninformed by the advent of uncapping because they feel there is nothing they can do to affect the law, in any case, and they do not see much they can do or need to do in their own lives to prepare for a far-off event

*Kevin Gray 1989, personal correspondence.

that may or may not happen as planned. There appeared to be some evidence for this in the Gray study (1989).

In a discussion with Mr. Gray, we pointed out that his responding population was a mix of tenured faculty and other higher education employees. Further, all ages were com-mingled, lumping together those who would reach the com-pulsory retirement age while it would still be in effect with those young enough to profit from uncapping. In a letter, Gray replied as follows:

> . . . *you raised an interesting question: If respondents who indicated they had been affected in SOME way by the 1986 ADEA amendments were treated as one group, and if respondents' ages were taken into account, might not a dif-ferential impact on tenured faculty and other employees appear?*
>
> *Indeed that turned out to be the case. While among respondents aged 62 to 70, occupation and the effect of the 1986 amendments were independent, this was not true in the 55 to 61 age group. Among these respondents, 20 per-cent of the tenured faculty said they had been affected in some way, compared with 10 percent of other employees. This age-by-occupation was significant (at the $p = .0432$ level).* *

Gray's detailed response indicated that faculty members who will be among the earliest to be affected by uncapping are most aware of the ADEA amendments' potential effect on their career. Also, the above suggests caution in interpreting studies that do not examine differences in faculty members' retirement intentions as a function of awareness and under-standing of the potential impact of uncapping.

The Role of Emeriti Faculty
Much of the information about emeritus postretirement activi-ties includes all retired faculty. Kellams and Chronister (1988) studied one aspect of the question and found that retirees (average age of retirement in their population was 62) remain active for many years. Of the respondents, 81 percent said they continued in academic professional activities such as part-

*Kevin Gray 1989, personal correspondence.

time teaching, research, professional reading and writing, working with graduate students, supervising student teachers, and consulting.

Trice (1981) found that professors wanted a partial continuation of a work role similar to the preretirement role, while at the same time they indicated a satisfaction with the retirement experience. Her sample was taken from emeritus professors at AAU institutions.

Some emeriti form associations and meet periodically about common concerns. There is, for example, The Ohio State University Retirees Association, with dues, bylaws, and officers.

Southern Illinois University at Carbondale created an Emeritus College that, among other things, established a scholarship endowment for undergraduates, created a monthly public affairs forum for the community, conducted six-week preretirement seminars, arranged for guest lecturers in classes, recruited volunteers for tutors and mentors, and worked to develop a retirement housing complex (Auerbach 1986c).

Appley (1987) wrote in *Academy Notes*, a publication that reported on emeriti developments and served as a clearinghouse, of the annual Western Conference on Retirement in Colleges and Universities and the organizational activities of emeriti on campuses around the country, including the University of Washington, University of Massachusetts, and Eckerd College. (An Academy of Senior Professionals is planned at Eckerd, with campus residential housing and a research retirement complex.)

Emeriti have been active for many years at the University of California at Los Angeles and the University of Southern California. Their emeriti and retirement centers and associations have served as models for other institutions. The first systemwide emeriti association in the nation was founded in the 19-campus California State University (CSU) system. This Emeritus and Retired Faculty Association (ERFA) has given impetus to the formation of local campus retired faculty organizations, has collected the names and addresses of the emeriti of the system, and is in the process of developing a talent bank. ERFA has gained representation on the CSU Academic Senate and in the California Faculty Association, the system's faculty collective bargaining agent, including standing subcommittees on emeriti and retirement issues.

The USC Emeriti Center has sponsored several annual West Coast Conferences on Retirement in Colleges and Universities, promoting an exchange of information and a coalition or conference of organizations of the region. This may eventually lead to a network of emeritus faculty organizations around the country (Albert 1986).

Faculty Members' View of Emeritus Status
A study of Canadian faculty in Ontario (B. Hansen 1985) suggested that, contrary to the findings of Chronister and Kepple (1987), early retirement is viewed as one of the least attractive options to faculty. Hansen found that over a 10-year period approximately 125 Ontario faculty elected to take retirement. This averaged about 10 per year from a faculty complement of between 10,000 and 11,000 (in percentage terms about 0.1 percent per year). Universities in Ontario have been permitted to retire faculty at age 65, although that is now being tested in the courts.

In speculating on why early retirement has been so unattractive to faculty, Hansen's instinctive answer was that academics have jobs that give them a lot of satisfaction. Faculty do not easily abandon congenial work prematurely when the costs of abandonment in financial and psychological terms are high. This seems to be supported in Ontario by the evidence of greater use of reduced time, leave without pay, and assignment to other institutions, which allow faculty to remain in familiar work situations but with reduced commitments, or with a guarantee to return later (B. Hansen 1985).

The responses of Canadian faculty members to questions about early retirement are instructive in terms of what they want when they envision having emeritus status. A selection of quotes from the study is illustrative of the point:

> *Professor, Arts, age 54, . . . I like what I'm doing and am not at all enthusiastic about retiring early. In fact, I'd most like to keep going at reduced load after 65—visiting professor, etc. . . . People live too long nowadays in good health to be thrown out at 65—perhaps into poverty.*
>
> *Professor, Drama, age 56, . . . In the discipline in which I work, a faculty member's value increases cumulatively, on the whole, with age and experience . . . . His/her last years of teaching [are] probably the most valuable of all. Therefore, my interest in schemes for early replacement or retirement of staff is limited to exceptional cases of waning or otherwise unsatisfactory performance.*

Professor, Communications, age 51, . . . I like my work and would prefer reduced responsibility rather than full retirement.

Associate Professor, Industrial Engineering, age 57, . . . First choice—half-time appointment if full benefits and good pension adjustments were included. Second choice, early retirement if good pension provisions were available (p. 291).

Faculty members who have written about emeritus status seem to point to an active professional lifestyle, not unlike their working life but a bit less hectic, with reduced pressure from classes and students and more time to devote to travel and their own professional interests and research. If this is accurate, it might mean that institutions could plan to put real meaning and distinctiveness into the rank, reserving it for the most active, interested faculty. And faculty might be more likely to treat the rank as a meaningful opportunity to make additional contributions rather than simply an honorific title.

Other considerations for faculty may be more mundane. For example, some are ready to retire but feel they cannot because of loss of health benefits that they or family members depend on. If emeritus status in some way helped in continuing health, and perhaps other benefits, they might retire immediately. We do know that, among TIAA institutions, many colleges and universities do not continue retired employees in their group health insurance plans. Of those that do, most have some eligibility requirements, and most require the retired faculty member to pay either the full cost or most of the cost (TIAA-CREF 1988a).

An informative way of investigating what faculty want when they envision emeritus status is to look at what colleges offer to entice older scholars to retire. Some colleges and universities are finding ways to keep faculty active in retirement, whether the motivation is to retire them or to retain the services of those they would rather not lose. These colleges offer faculty what they want: office and laboratory space, secretarial help, library and parking privileges, and opportunities to teach and work with students part time. One of the biggest fears faculty have about retirement is that they will be cut off from colleagues and students and the rich intellectual environment they are used to; avoiding this separation is what is wanted in emeritus status (Blum 1988; Mangan 1988).

Some institutions also provide an opportunity to retire gradually, allowing faculty to reduce their workload gradually over time. Others support emeritus associations that provide privileges on campus as well as organize social and academic events, lectures, lunches, and seminars that appeal to emeritus faculty and keep them involved and up-to-date. Albert (1986, p. 24) writes about a redefinition or reinterpretation of retirement and emeritus status. As chair, Committee E of the California Conference of AAUP, he carried out a charge from that conference to make recommendations concerning the role of emeriti in university life. The document was characterized as an emeriti bill of rights, and it begins with the concept of conferring emeritus status as an act of recognition of long and meritorious service, seeing it as an earned rank that carries with it certain rights.

Among the emeritus rights, paraphrased from Albert's list, are items that one would ordinarily expect, such as pre-retirement information, instruction, and counseling on financial and social issues associated with retirement; receipt of news about the institution; access to postretirement counseling and guidance; faculty club membership; faculty dining privileges; use of campus recreational and social facilities; admission to athletic, dramatic, film, musical, and other cultural events of the institution; credit union services; access to college and alumni travel programs; and retirement faculty identification cards. These would be expected to involve little or no incremental cost to the institution and may well be available to all retired faculty.

A second group of rights and responsibilities, in addition to those above, would be a step up in terms of institutional cost and commitment and in terms of restricting such rights to emeritus faculty. They would include emeritus faculty listings in college directories and catalogs, emeritus identification cards providing library privileges, emeritus faculty parking privileges, receipt of campus publications and notices, departmental mail addresses, participation in ceremonies and academic processions, attendance at faculty meetings and faculty functions, opportunity to audit courses, use of the college guest house, faculty discounts at the university press and book store, and the opportunity to teach part time if needed.

Emeritus status of this nature would certainly be of value to faculty yet not involve a great deal of commitment on the part of either the individual or the institution. Where costs are involved, they may well be borne by the individual if employed faculty are also charged, e.g., parking or campus events. In this case, costs to the institution may be minimal.

The third area of emeritus rights is more substantial, and institutions may limit items to a group of emeritus faculty who want to continue their campus teaching, research, and other activities and who are welcomed in that role by the institution. This emeritus rank would include the availability of negotiated teaching and advising assignments, laboratory and other research resources, departmental office space, a telephone, secretarial services, computers, word processors, stationery, supplies, mailing privileges, and other resources. This rank of emeritus faculty would, in pursuing research, have the right to receive and administer grants, contracts, awards, and other funded research projects. As emeritus faculty, they would receive help in producing scholarly publications, in making research and other grant proposals, and in making presentations at professional meetings. They would be able to serve on thesis and dissertation committees, on departmental committees, on campus or state faculty committees, or on the campus speaker roster, to serve the institution in a variety of advisory or consultant capacities, and to participate in seminars, colloquia, lectures, and other scholarly meetings (Albert 1986).

Finally, there are a number of "rights" emeriti seek with respect to associating with one another. Albert (1986) mentions the right to establish an association of emeritus faculty on campus, to establish an emeritus faculty center on campus, to use campus meeting rooms for association meetings, and to have representation of emeritus faculty, or their association, on senate and faculty councils.

Another indication of faculty desires comes from the AAUP position, which is moving toward recognition of phased retirement plans that enable faculty to negotiate reductions in services and salary acceptable to them and the institution.

Each institution should help retired faculty members and administrators remain a part of the academic community, and facilitate timely retirement, by providing, where possible, such amenities as a mail address, library privileges, office space, faculty club membership, the institution's publications, secretarial help, administration of grants, research facilities, faculty dining and parking privileges, and par-

One of the biggest fears faculty have about retirement is that they will be cut off from colleagues and students and the rich intellectual environment...

ticipation in convocations and academic processions. Institutions that confer emeritus status should do so in accordance with standards determined by the faculty and administration (AAUP 1988, p. 38).

The Emeritus Status and Collective Bargaining

The relationship between collective bargaining and the status of emeritus faculty is one that is limited at present, but that may change. Some assert that as faculties age and as uncapping becomes a reality, faculty unions will be dominated by older, senior professors who will push for increasing benefits at the end of the career line rather than at the beginning, thus leading to emeritus status as an important collective bargaining issue, along with wages and other conditions of employment. In a limited number of institutions, emeritus status is referred to and sometimes defined in a collective bargaining agreement.

On the other hand, collective bargaining for the whole faculty of an institution appears to have been weakened recently by a number of factors, including the *Yeshiva* case. And in those institutions where one would expect the greatest interest in a continued professional relationship with the institution, collective bargaining has been least successful, e.g., the large research and graduate universities (Blum 1989b).

The move to organize part-time faculty continues strongly (Jennings 1988). If emeriti occupy a significant number of part-time positions, they could well become enmeshed in collective bargaining.

The Changing Role of Emeritus Faculty

There is little evidence that the role of emeritus faculty is changing, principally because the evidence would have to be based on research comparisons over time. There has not, up to this time, been the interest needed to generate that research. The study of the authors may be a beginning of change, however, because that research can be done periodically to ascertain if changes are occurring (Mauch, Birch, and Matthews 1989a, 1989b).

Some are writing about a changing role, and that may be a sign of transformation to come (AAUP 1988; Albert 1986; COFHE 1989). Emeritus faculty could become the fastest-growing group in higher education, and a steadily aging, active faculty is a reality today.

This development is beginning to attract notice in the academic world. Four changes are clear. First, the number of emeriti faculty is large and growing. Second, emeriti are becoming more assertive about what they look upon as their rights (Albert 1986). Third, emeriti are attaining recognition in policy statements of major professional organizations (AAUP 1988). And fourth, emeriti are organizing themselves and conducting conferences with themes arising from self-interest (Albert 1986; Auerbach 1986a, 1986c; Blum 1988). Taken together, these moves seem to set the stage for more visible and, possibly, a more influential role for emeriti in higher education in the future.

The Relationship between Uncapping and Emeritus Status

First, if uncapping swells the ranks of aging faculty at some or even many institutions, the emeritus rank may provide a way to help faculty retire while retaining what they and their institutions most want.

Second, even without a swelling of the ranks, the increasing number and intellectual vigor of retired faculty mean that there is a valuable national resource that could be retained by awarding faculty emeritus status (valuable faculty who are no longer paid) rather than retiring faculty (faculty who are no longer seen or heard from).

Fifteen college and university presidents were interviewed during the pretest of an inquiry form about emeritus status (Mauch, Birch, and Matthews 1989a). Without exception, each president sometime during the interview spoke warmly of one or more current senior faculty members who, everyone wished, could stay on forever. The relationship between uncapping and emeritus status suggested below could allow those college and university presidents to come as close as is humanly possible to realizing that wish.

This proposed relationship between uncapping and emeritus status is consistent with and builds upon recommendations of the AAUP (1988) and of various emeriti representatives (Albert 1986; Blum 1988; Mangan 1988). Meritorious teachers and researchers on the campus should be identified before age 55 and interviewed concerning their current ideas about retirement and about their own retirement plans. Such interviews should be repeated every year or two. Pains should be taken to let the faculty members know that the institution

wants them to stay as long as they feel they can be productive and enjoy campus life. It should be made clear that it is institutional policy to arrange individualized leaves and reduced loads, at mutually agreeable times. Each such arrangement would be phased on a personal time schedule through step-by-step decreasing commitments, if that is what the faculty member wishes, leading to full retirement. The move to less than a full-time schedule would also involve transfer to emeritus professor status and adjustments in salary, continued tenure in a less-than-full-time position, negotiated alterations in benefits, as well as any other considerations important to the particular faculty member. Moreover, it would be understood that the part-time arrangement could be reviewed periodically at the request of either party.

Central to this proposed relationship between uncapping and emeritus status is the concept of the emeritus professorship as a *bona fide* rank, equal to the rank of full professor, and further distinguished by being a recognition of long-term and high-quality performance. The emeritus rank would be reserved for those academics who, having earned it, wish to continue their professional and scholarly pursuits on an individually negotiated less-than-full-time schedule.

Not all faculty planning retirement would seek such an arrangement, nor would all merit it. The main thrust of the suggested relationship would be to help keep as many as possible of the most productive faculty members active and happy in their later career years, thus benefiting themselves and the institution and accomplishing that at a more reasonable financial cost to the college or university.

Naturally, specific details of the suggested relationship would vary from campus to campus. A framework for fitting the emeritus rank into the existing tenured rank structure is discussed later. Accommodations would need to be made, of course, and already existing policies and practices might need minor amendments. The central theme of individualization, though, ought to remain intact.

Summary

On the basis of both theory and research, it appears that faculty will seek role continuity long into their later years. There are few studies available to guide institutions in setting policy in preparation for uncapping, and there are no clear trends with respect to how long—or to what age—faculty can be expected to work. Institutions of higher education need additional data in anticipation of uncapping. In addition to increasing life span, a number of recent changes are likely to affect faculty retirement decisions. There are assumptions about faculty working until later ages and patterns by types of institutions, but there is little evidence to support or reject these assumptions. Options at retirement for individual faculty vary greatly.

CURRENTS OF CHANGE

Calls for Change

Congress called for a study under the guidance of the National Academy of Sciences "to analyze the potential consequences of the elimination of mandatory retirement on institutions of higher education," with the findings to be reported in 1991. As of this writing, that study is under way under the direction of Ralph E. Gomory, chair of the Committee on Mandatory Retirement in Higher Education.

In addition, a report of the AAUP (1987b) pointed out that very little useful information exists on current retirement policies in higher education. Soon after, AAUP (1988) prepared a new revision of a joint statement originally issued in 1950 entitled, "Statement of Principles on Academic Retirement and Insurance Plans." In effect, the statement endorses and recommends new policies for institutions of higher education.

Recently, a limited number of studies have begun to investigate aspects of the potential consequences of mandatory retirement on institutions of higher education referred to by Congress (Chronister and Kepple 1987; Dooris and Lozier 1987; Gray 1989; Lozier and Dooris 1988–89).

In another recent development, Albert Rees, recently retired president of the Alfred P. Sloan Foundation, became director, Project on Faculty Retirement, and senior economist at Princeton University. Sharon P. Smith is the project's associate director. This project is gathering data from approximately 40 institutions on the demographics of the tenured faculty in the arts and sciences by broad disciplinary groups. The data will cover the timing of retirement and the relative attributes of late and early retirees, concentrating solely on arts and sciences faculty. The list of participating schools is not nor was it intended to be random or representative of all institutions of higher education. The population is largely made up of leading research universities and selective liberal arts colleges. Attention will be focused on schools where the advisory group believes the most severe impact of uncapping will occur, and these will be compared with similar schools that have been uncapped. Data are now being collected and analyzed and a report prepared.*

Because the literature on a number of questions was very limited, the authors initiated a study of emeritus policies in

---

*Sharon P. Smith 1989, personal correspondence.

two populations of institutions of higher education. One is made up of degree-granting institutions of higher education in Pennsylvania, the other of members of the AAU.

The AAU institutions were solicited because the responses would reflect the policies of the leading research universities in the United States and Canada. Information was solicited from all 58 members of AAU, and survey responses were received from 38, or 66 percent, of the AAU population.

Pennsylvania was included because it was accessible and because it has a wide variety of public and private institutions of higher education in all categories, including four AAU institutions. Survey instruments were sent to all 154 degree-granting Pennsylvania institutions, and responses were received from 77.

The four Pennsylvania universities belonging to the AAU were included in both populations; thus, the two populations were not completely distinct.

Directed to presidents, the survey instrument sought information concerning the role of emeritus faculty on the campuses. The instrument requested institutions to provide information on emeritus status; collective bargaining agreements; tenured faculty; retirement policies and practices; and privileges, responsibilities, practices, services, rights, and professional opportunities sometimes extended by colleges and universities to emeritus faculty.

Personal letters were sent by the president of the University of Pittsburgh Senate to presidents of degree-granting institutions in Pennsylvania. AAU members were encouraged to respond by a memo sent from the Office of Management Information and Policy Analysis to AAU Data Exchange members, as well as by a letter from the president of the University of Pittsburgh Senate.

Institutions with Compulsory Retirement
As we indicated earlier, by 1980 some institutions of higher education had already begun to uncap, or perhaps never had a compulsory retirement age. The U.S. Department of Labor study (1982) found that 52 percent of the institutions (employing 68 percent of all faculty) it studied had a policy of retirement at age 70 or above, while 20 percent (employing 12 percent of the faculty) had no retirement age cap at all. At the time of the DOL survey, tenured faculty could be forced to retire at age 65.

The Lozier-Dooris study (1988–89) found that the vast majority of institutions had already adopted 70 as the mandatory retirement age, even during the years when they were not required to do so. These two authors also projected a continuation of past retirement age patterns, because they see little evidence of change and they find some evidence that actual retirement age of faculty has been influenced little by changes in the mandatory retirement age.

The COFHE study (1989) did find a slight rise in retirement age, but the COFHE population is a rather select group and not necessarily representative of all faculty.

In a study of AAU institutions, Mauch, Birch, and Matthews (1989a) found that 84 percent of the responding institutions had a compulsory retirement age for tenured faculty. Six of the responding AAU universities reported that they did not have a compulsory retirement age. For those that did, 76 percent reported 70 as the age of compulsory retirement, one reported age 71, and seven failed to report any age.

In Pennsylvania institutions (Mauch, Birch, and Matthews 1989b), 53 percent reported a compulsory retirement age. Twenty-three percent said they did not have a compulsory retirement age, and 23 percent failed to answer this question. Of the 53 percent, almost all reported age 70.

Thus, it appears that in 1978 when the mandatory retirement age was raised to 70 by law, many institutions of higher education also raised the age to 70 for tenured faculty, even though they were not required to do so until July 1, 1982. Now, however, under similar circumstance (institutions could follow the lead of the law and remove the mandatory age requirement altogether), it appears they are not doing so.

There are several alternative explanations for this. One is that there may be little pressure from faculty to do so. Also, there may be some hope that Congress will change its mind about ending the exception for tenured faculty in higher education at the end of 1993. Another explanation might be that institutions are as yet not facing a faculty shortage and they still want to continue early retirement and other programs encouraging faculty to retire to make room for young scholars on the faculty.

Institutions Awarding Emeritus Status

Our own study indicates that all of the reporting AAU institutions use the term "emeritus" to designate the status of cer-

. . . 84 percent of the responding institutions had a compulsory retirement age for tenured faculty.

tain faculty and that 80 percent of the Pennsylvania institutions of higher education do so also. Although the term means different things to different institutions, it is not a term used to designate all faculty retirees in 79 percent of the AAU institutions or in 88 percent of the Pennsylvania institutions.

In many cases, the emeritus award is conferred by trustees. This is true in 34 percent of the AAU institutions, while 24 percent rely on a vote of the faculty to confer emeritus status and 13 percent reserve this authority for the president. For the Pennsylvania institutions, the percentages are 39 percent for trustees, 16 percent for presidents, and 9 percent for vote of the faculty.

Sixty percent of AAU members and 49 percent of the Pennsylvania institutions issue a letter or certificate as a part of conferring emeritus rank.

Criteria Used to Appoint Emeriti

The most common criterion is tenure status. Half (50 percent) of the AAU universities and 43 percent of the Pennsylvania institutions require tenure status for the conferring of emeritus rank.

Next is the requirement of a specified number of years of full-time employment at the institution. This is the case at 47 percent of the AAU institutions and 39 percent of the Pennsylvania colleges and universities.

Evidence of distinguished service is required for the awarding of emeritus status in 42 percent of AAU institutions and 53 percent of the Pennsylvania institutions.

Most of the colleges and universities—92 percent of the AAU members and 74 percent of the Pennsylvania institutions—said the criteria and procedures for the award of emeritus rank were essentially the same throughout the institution.

Faculty Privileges

The literature is limited on this question. One researcher (Holden 1985) reports in her seminal work, done largely with universities and four-year colleges, that only a small number of institutions provided office and clerical services to retired faculty. While virtually all institutions in her study granted library privileges, about 45 percent never provided secretarial, office, or laboratory facilities to them. About 25 percent of the institutions would grant these services and facilities upon special request, and about 15 percent granted them only to emeritus professors and only 5 percent to retirees. Yet the majority of the older faculty employed at these institutions wanted to and expected to continue professional involvement after retirement.

There are, of course, costs associated with providing services to retired or emeritus faculty. Some privileges, such as those provided on a space-available basis or those for which a fee is collected, may cost the institution little. Others, such as space, computer services, labs, supplies, and secretarial service, clearly have a cost. A comprehensive cost-benefit analysis of providing an array of privileges to faculty as an alternative to remaining in full-time employment is recommended. The literature on this subject is severely limited.

In terms of the privileges accorded emeritus and retired faculty in the AAU large research universities, the authors' study found a number that were quite common. Table 1 lists the 12 privileges (from a list of 50) that 50 percent or more of the AAU institutions reported applied to retired faculty. Also listed are the percentages that applied to all faculty and to emeritus faculty only. Thus, the table indicates that 87 percent of the AAU universities provided pre-retirement information to all retired faculty and none limited this privilege to emeriti only. Also, 79 percent extended regular faculty library privileges to all retired faculty, and 13 percent limited this privilege to emeriti only.

Table 2 lists the five privileges (from a list of 50) that 50 percent or more of the Pennsylvania institutions reported applied to retired faculty. Also listed are the percentages that applied to all faculty and to emeritus faculty only. Thus, the table indicates that 78 percent of the Pennsylvania colleges and universities permitted all retired faculty to remain on college mailing lists if they wished. Three institutions (4 percent) provided this privilege only to emeriti. Seventy-one percent extended regular faculty library privileges to all retired faculty, and 9 percent limited this privilege to emeriti only.

The Reemployment of Emeritus Faculty
Thirty-four percent of AAU universities reported that retired faculty are offered opportunities to teach as needed; an additional 37 percent said that such opportunities are offered "informally on an individual basis." This means that somewhat more than two-thirds of the AAU institutions reporting can offer opportunities for retired faculty to teach to some degree,

however limited; in 8 percent, such opportunities are limited to emeriti only. Most (66 percent) responded that retired faculty are not given preference for part-time teaching jobs.

TABLE 1

COMMON PRIVILEGES ACCORDED EMERITUS AND RETIRED FACULTY IN AAU INSTITUTIONS

PRIVILEGE	% ALL RETIRED FACULTY	% EMERITUS ONLY
Preretirement information is provided	87	0
Have regular faculty library privileges	79	13
May use campus recreational and social facilities	79	10
Are charged as regular faculty for cultural events	76	10
Are given identification cards or the equivalent	76	10
Have access to college or alumni travel programs	71	3
Have access to college credit union services	68	0
Preretirement counseling is provided	66	0
May audit academic courses	63	8
May remain on college mailing list if they wish	60	16
Have parking privileges other faculty have	50	26
Receive campus publications and notices	50	16

Source: Mauch, Birch, and Matthews 1989a.

TABLE 2

COMMON PRIVILEGES ACCORDED EMERITUS AND RETIRED FACULTY IN PENNSYLVANIA INSTITUTIONS

PRIVILEGE	% ALL RETIRED FACULTY	% EMERITUS ONLY
May remain on college mailing list	78	4
Have regular faculty library privileges	71	9
Receive campus publications and notices	57	12
May use campus recreational and social facilities	54	9
Preretirement information is provided	53	0

Source: Mauch, Birch, and Matthews 1989b.

In terms of reemployment of retired tenured faculty, 92 percent of the AAU institutions indicated they make provisions for reemployment, as needed, on term contracts. Such reemployment would be in a number of categories, not only teaching.

Forty-three percent of Pennsylvania institutions reported that retired faculty are offered opportunities to teach as needed. An additional 32 percent said that such opportunities are offered "informally on an individual basis." This means that almost two-thirds of the Pennsylvania institutions offer opportunities for retired faculty to teach as needed. Forty-eight percent reported that retired faculty are not given preference for part-time teaching jobs.

Fifty-five percent of Pennsylvania institutions indicated they provide for reemployment in some capacity of retired tenured faculty, as needed, on term contracts.

Emeritus Faculty as Part of the "Working" Faculty

Predicting future enrollments, availability of faculty, and likely age of faculty retirement is less than an exact science, but the prospects for uncapping of the mandatory retirement age have made the need for solid data more critical. Even when there is more solid information, planning efforts will have a margin of error. Neither the data generated by the surveys of AAU members and Pennsylvania degree-granting institutions nor the results of the literature search can furnish more than general guidelines and suggestions concerning new data needed for the process of planning for the decade ahead.

There is evidence that in the decade of the 1990s there will not be a glut of qualified faculty (Bowen and Schuster 1986; Lozier and Dooris 1987). The coming decades may be a period during which higher education will continue to cope with costs that rise at a rate above the general increase in cost of living.

While there seems to be agreement as to the trend of faculty members' retiring in increasing numbers, many faculty will not want to withdraw totally from active work. They will welcome an opportunity to continue what they have been doing but at their own pace—and for some, under newly negotiated terms of employment. The possibilities are with us for a new form of working rank for the emeritus professor in which competence and experience built up over the years will continue to be utilized at a price higher education can afford. The new emeritus professor may not be expecting a continuation of the salary—or the pressures and responsibilities—experienced prior to being elevated to emeritus rank.

The new emeritus rank should offer such flexibility that it will prove to be an attractive option, one that does not deprive higher education of the continued services of productive faculty. The change can be one that leads from a historical "emeritus professor" image—honorific, distinguished, retired—to a new image of working rank, equally distinguished but accenting productivity as well.

The Emeritus Professor Status in Collective Bargaining Contracts

The AAUP provided texts of provisions on emeritus faculty contained in AAUP collective bargaining contracts in effect as of January 7, 1988. These contracts are excerpted below. Some are available through ERIC (AAUP 1983a, 1983b, 1984, 1987a). If they are representative of such contracts, it appears that the references to emeritus status in collective bargaining agreements vary greatly in both meaning and substance.

The fact that the term "emeritus" appears at all in present-day collective bargaining contracts could be significant in itself. In the eyes of some faculties and administrators, it is thereby acknowledged to be a topic worthy of some weight in balancing higher education employer-employee relations. Also, clearly there are many other contracts with affiliates of the NEA and the AFT that were not examined, so there is no way of being sure exactly how widely the emeritus concept extends in collective bargaining contracts.

The contracts that were reviewed, however, spoke in two ways about emeritus faculty: how emeriti are defined and what privileges or benefits are associated with emeritus status. The variance both in definitions and in privileges and benefits is illustrated below. They are listed roughly in order of the prominence given to the topic in the contract.

Union County College

All retired faculty members shall have emeritus status, and all retired faculty members, at their request, shall be listed in the faculty directory, shall be invited to participate in college ceremonies, may attend faculty meetings without the right to vote, shall have library privileges, and shall have the same discounts on purchases at college facilities as faculty members (AAUP 1984).

Bloomfield College

A faculty member who retires from Bloomfield College after at least seven years of full-time service at the institution shall be eligible for emeritus status at the rank held at the time of retirement (AAUP 1983a).

Utica College

A faculty member shall have completed a minimum of 10 years of service at Utica College to be eligible for emeritus status recommendation, and the faculty member should be in good standing at Utica College (AAUP 1987a).

Wilberforce University

The title "emeritus" is a signal honor that may be bestowed only by the Board of Trustees. A recommendation for emeritus status shall originate at the academic division level. The recommendation shall be forwarded to the vice president for academic affairs, who shall forward the recommendation and accompanying approval or disapproval to the president. The president shall consider it for approval and if favorable, shall forward the recommendation to the Board of Trustees for final action.

The basic criteria for emeritus status shall be 15 consecutive honorable years of service at Wilberforce University, professional achievement, outstanding work on university committees, and participation in the functioning of the university (AAUP 1983b).

Central State University

Emeritus status is the highest earned faculty rank awarded by the Board of Trustees to retired tenured faculty members. Recommendations for the awarding of emeritus status shall be initiated by the department chair after consultation with members of the department and shall be forwarded by the prescribed university procedure to the dean, the Committee on Promotion and Tenure, the vice president for academic affairs, and the president. It is understood that the retired faculty member shall have made a significant contribution to the university and/or served at least 10 years at Central State University.

An emeritus faculty member will be entitled to the use of an office and research facilities, including laboratories, provided he or she uses it regularly and there is sufficient space available. Emeriti will also be entitled, on the same basis as other faculty members, to use of the library, tickets to university functions, use of recreational facilities, use of parking facilities, remission of all instructional fees, a mailbox, listing in the university catalog and campus directory, secretarial assistance in typing manuscripts, stationery and similar supplies, access to the computer center, institutional support for university proposals submitted to funding agencies, and assistance in defraying costs incurred when giving papers or acting as session chairs at scholarly meetings and when publishing articles in scholarly periodicals.*

Northern Michigan University
The Northern Michigan University contracts for 1987–88 and 1988–89 called for retired faculty members to receive a membership card in the Retirees Association, which entitles them to a list of benefits, including free enrollment in university courses, use of the library, parking at no charge, and complimentary tickets to most athletic, dramatic, and cultural events. The contracts provided that "persons with emeritus title may march in academic processions, [participate in] commencement, and represent the university on appointment at academic ceremonies of other institutions." Another provision said, "Emeritus groups will have access to campus rooms and facilities for meetings and reunions and opportunity to establish an emeriti association on the same basis as other community groups."*

Examination of these collective bargaining contracts in general reveals that some contain provisions setting forth benefits for retired faculty. Several contracts use the term "emeritus." Others make no mention of the term. It is not unusual for a contract to use the terms "emeritus" and "retired" interchangeably. The distinction between emeritus and retired faculty is not clear when one considers the entire sample of contracts reviewed. However, where a distinction was made between faculty retirees in general and those awarded emeritus standing, the emeritus faculty tended to be particularly recognized for length and quality of service

*Robert Kreiser 1989, personal correspondence.

to the institution and often were made eligible for special collegial and institutional considerations that encouraged them
to continue to be active in scholarly work in their departments
and on campus.

Revising Tenure in Light of Uncapping

The AAUP Executive Committee has confirmed as a high-
priority issue "maintaining the tenure system following the
abolition of mandatory retirement" (AAUP 1988). The committee's action may be quite timely, for there is no doubt that
proposals for revisions in the tenure system have been stim-
ulated by the likelihood of uncapping. Most proposed changes
are in the direction of either outright abolition or the intro-
duction of fixed-term contracts to the system (Heller 1986;
Ruebhausen 1989; Ruebhausen and Woodruff 1986).

*. . . institutions
will have to be
more rigorous
and fair in
assessing the
professional
effectiveness
of all employ-
ees, not just
faculty . . .*

Also, the 1988 "Statement of Principles on Academic Retirement and Insurance Plans" encourages plans that enable individual faculty members, at their initiative, to embark on
phased retirement schemes, with services and salaries adjusted
in ways acceptable to all parties involved. It is not clear, however, from this statement whether the phased retirement plan
envisioned is to constitute a phased relinquishing of tenure
at the same time and on the same schedule.

Another move significant to the status of tenure in its historical form is the inclusion in the 1988 "Statement" of a new
category of possible tenure violation through involuntary termination. In this case, if a faculty member is caused to retire
under the existing law at age 70 and another faculty member
whose birthday is one day later may stay on because of the
lapse of the law, some negotiated accommodation may prove
both appropriate and advisable. In addition, if tenured faculty
in the future are pressured to retire or are frequently found
to be unsatisfactory at age 70 and beyond, and if there seems
to be a pattern, it could become a tenure violation issue.

If tenure were to be revised by an institution as a result of
uncapping, it might result in such a divisive and acrimonious
situation that it would seriously cripple the institution. Such
a unilateral action would also strengthen the hand of any local
or potential union on campus. And finally, it should be clear
that such changes would not alter the fact that untenured
faculty and other employees are, in any case, legally protected
from age discrimination in employment.

Tenure at present is deeply entrenched in our system of higher education and in the minds of many is closely related to the concept and practice of academic freedom. In fact, in the study of the AAU member universities, all reported written policies governing tenure. In addition, 78 percent of the Pennsylvania institutions said that they have written policies governing tenure, while 21 percent failed to answer the question. Only one respondent reported having no written policy (Mauch, Birch, and Matthews 1989a, 1989b).

If the rest of the country is similar to Pennsylvania in this regard, it means that about four out of five colleges and universities have written tenure policies; thus, one might conclude that a similar proportion, at least, has a tenure system.

In another recent study, Gray (1989) found that 80 percent of the faculty employees in his population of higher education institutions were tenured, while Mortimer, Bagshaw, and Masland (1985) reported that 94 percent of four-year colleges and universities have a tenure system and that about 57 percent of all full-time faculty at these institutions are tenured. Thus, it would seem difficult to revise tenure in a way that is not acceptable to faculty, absent some dramatic change in the system.

Summary

In view of the possible change in long-standing temporal connections among a fixed retirement age, the schedule of institutional contributions to retirement funds, and the tenure system, it can be anticipated that there will be a period of uncertainty and readjustment. It is possible that the outcome may include at least minor changes in the tenure system, though not the rejection of the system itself. One of the possible changes is a negotiated agreement to alter tenure for those who wish to transfer to an emeritus status.

In any case, some attractive alternatives that encourage voluntary retirement in a cost-saving way and that allow tenured faculty who wish to do so to continue a productive relationship with the academy are becoming more necessary (Ruebhausen 1988). Without such alternatives, the perception that the elimination of mandatory retirement will leave the institution in the hands of an aging faculty that each year eats up an increasing share of the resources will only intensify the public policy debate over the future of tenure.

In addition, institutions will have to be more rigorous and fair in assessing the professional effectiveness of all employees, not just faculty, not just tenured faculty, and certainly not just tenured faculty who have passed what was the mandatory retirement age. The wise institution will indeed get its house in order before December 31, 1993.

FINDINGS: POLICY AND PRACTICE CONSIDERATIONS

Timely Interpretation of the Emeritus Rank

Attention has already been called to the probability of total uncapping as of January 1, 1994. If a new conception of the emeritus rank is to play a part in higher education institutions' adjustment to the abolition of a mandatory retirement age for tenured faculty, any changes should be set in place soon.

There are other reasons, too, for a sense of timeliness. Moves are afoot to organize part-time faculty for collective bargaining. Emeritus faculty organizations are also forming, quite apart from collective bargaining groups. Some existing professional organizations are beginning to mount advocacy campaigns for retired and emeritus faculty. University senates are showing increased interest in the emeritus rank, particularly in its rights and privileges.

Up to now, the situation has been fluid; positions have not firmed. There appears to be both flexibility and a cooperative spirit among the parties influenced by uncapping. Mutually agreeable and individually protective solutions are being sought to what many see as potentially vexing problems. These are the circumstances that make a current discussion of a new interpretation of the emeritus rank very appropriate.

The Relationship between the New Emeritus Rank and Existing Ranks

The following conception of the emeritus status as a rank, integrated into the conventional working rank structure of assistant, associate, and full professor reflects a proposal first introduced into the literature by Mirel (1977). It also includes components suggested by Albert (1986) and by Mauch, Birch, and Matthews (1989a, 1989b).

The professor emeritus rank would be awarded in the same fashion as are other earned ranks. That is, a departmental recommendation would be processed through whatever committees and administrative and trustee procedures are used in the institution to award any other professorial rank.

It would be equivalent to full professor rank in all academic matters, yet certain qualifications would make it distinctively different from the full professorship in structural ways:

1. The emeritus professorship denotes that the faculty member is employed less than full time.
2. The emeritus professorship is an appointment at a fractional or part-time salary level.

3. The move to emeritus rank is a transfer rather than a promotion.
4. The conditions of employment at emeritus rank are individually negotiated between the faculty member and the institutional representative regarding tenure, contracts, schedule, duties, salary, benefits, prerequisites, and the like prior to transfer to emeritus status.
5. Most conditions of employment may be renegotiated upon the initiative of either party from year to year.
6. Any full professor with five or more years of service at the institution may apply for emeritus status after age 55.
7. Upon full retirement, the holder of emeritus rank may employ the title indefinitely.

Many faculty members would, no doubt, retire without transferring to emeritus rank first. Those faculty members would, by official act of the institution's trustees, be entitled to use the word "Retired" or the abbreviation "Ret." following the academic rank held just prior to retirement, as "A.B. Doe, Professor of Anthropology (Ret.), Erehorn University."

A Paradigm for Cost-Benefit Analysis

What makes it worthwhile for a college or university to deliberately encourage a faculty member of advanced years to continue in full- or part-time employment? Near the top of the list of reasons might be the gaining of prestigious publicity gained at little or no cost. If a very senior faculty member attracts grants and contracts that pay the professor's salary, support several young faculty members and graduate assistants, contribute a share to overhead, and pay for most supplies and travel while keeping the school's name in a favorable light in the public and academic media, a cost-benefit analysis is usually a superficial exercise. The case for encouraging that faculty member to stay on is a *prima facie* one.

But not all worthy scholarship yields such clear-cut and immediate dividends. Analysis of the advantages and costs if senior faculty members continue on campus in working roles more often calls for a careful weighing of the price against the product.

In the previous section, there is a listing of benefits emeriti value. In addition, it appears that college and university administrators see some benefits as more important than others (Mauch, Birch, and Matthews 1989a, 1989b). Clearly, benefits have economic and social value as well as economic and social costs.

It is instructive to think about the lists of benefits by comparing and contrasting their value to the institution and to the individual faculty member. Two examples:

1. *Benefit*: Emeritus faculty member has full access to library facilities.
   Value to Faculty Member: Opportunity to maintain contact with periodical and reference literature; use of a carrel; access to interlibrary loans, etc., to continue research, keep current, continue writing.
   Value to Institution: Suggestions about needed acquisitions; service on various library-related committees; model to students and junior faculty in use of library; possible gift of personal collection to library.
2. *Benefit*: Office in departmental area for emeritus professor.
   Value to Faculty Member: Feeling of recognition and belonging; convenience in carrying on work; stimulation *from* other faculty; office services available.
   Value to Institution: Stimulation *to* other faculty; service to department via committee work, lecturing advisement, mentoring junior faculty, fund raising, teaching, sponsored research, etc.

Denizens of academe know very well that almost every *quid* sooner or later has its *quo*. As the prospect of literally unending tenure moves closer to reality, perhaps the time has come to examine cost-benefit ratios in open discussion with individual prospective retirees and to work out mutually satisfactory accommodations.

Future Roles for Emeriti
A thread runs through the literature expressing desires of emeriti: to be kept informed, to be the recipient of important communications, to be treated as one of the academic community, an honored member of the academy. Many wish to continue, also, in the roles they have had, with modifications in pressure and time (Havighurst 1985; Holden 1985).

The benefit to the institution may be great. After all, faculty who have spent their lives at an institution often feel an emotional and academic attachment every bit as strong as alumni, and they want to keep in touch and to contribute their time and goods. They are certainly a valuable group of potential contributors. Of course, as we have said earlier, not all faculty have the same feeling toward their college, but those who do are a rich resource.

To determine roles of emeriti, it would seem essential to distinguish among retiring faculty in some way that would be appropriate and that would involve the institution and the faculty member. For example, in establishing a meaningful rank of emeritus professor, an institution may establish criteria to be met by those who wish to join that rank.

Clearly, not all would wish to join in such a scheme, nor would all be eligible. It may well be that there would be one group of retiring faculty who will take their retirement pay and never darken the door of the academy again. A second group will likely be those who, for whatever reasons, want only a minimum of continuing relationship.

The third group is the emeritus faculty, a group that does not look forward to retirement if that means being cut off permanently from colleagues, friends, the profession, research, students, reading, writing, analyzing, and debating issues and ideas. For some, this is the essence of life, or at least of professional life, and without it, life loses its meaning, its savor, and its richness. These are likely to be among the more committed and productive members of the faculty, and their productivity and commitment are not going to diminish at any arbitrary age. It should be possible to negotiate a mutually beneficial relationship with this group, to enable them to continue the productive life they so much want, and to enable the institution to continue to reap the benefits of that productive professional life. Such an agreement might well provide the perquisites listed earlier, and, after all, most of them do not present incremental costs to the institution.

The point is that starting soon, faculty can continue to receive all these perks, plus many more costly ones, as long as they wish and are able, simply by electing to delay retirement. Some of the perks will result in a benefit to the institution; e.g., listing of distinguished emeritus faculty in publications adds renown and attractiveness to the institution, and admitting emeriti to cultural, athletic, and academic events on the same basis as other faculty swells the ranks of what may otherwise be a poorly attended function and, if an admission charge is involved, swells the coffers as well.

Most important would be the role of emeriti in continuing their academic work without the pressure of full-time employment. Many faculty of retirement age are able to and would like to continue in their research (Blum 1988; Mangan 1988). Often this research brings prestige and funds to the institution, provides employment for assistants, provides support and scientific training and apprenticeship to graduate students, and provides a specific benefit to mankind or in some way points to a practical application that will help raise the quality of life.

Emeritus faculty are often excellent teachers because they have the time to spend with students, to mentor and monitor their progress, and to be a friend rather than an overseer. Emeritus faculty in our experience have often provided excellent help to graduate students in their scientific research and writings.

Where emeriti can serve as thesis or dissertation committee members, they often have the time and insight to devote to the student so that a successful result is obtained. Their wisdom and long experience can help students over some rough roads, a role often precluded by the pressures of being or becoming a recognized, tenured faculty member at a major university.

Emeritus faculty can be a rich resource for providing guest lectures in class, for delivering speeches, and for conducting workshops in their fields for community groups, groups of young students, and new faculty.

Not only are emeritus faculty effective at communicating institutional goals to students, faculty, and administrators; they are also often excellent ambassadors for the institution, presenting a picture of the institution that quietly and effectively communicates the institutional message. They are able and willing to help attract alumni interest, contacting alumni (often former students), soliciting alumni support, even in some cases approaching major donors. To many emeritus faculty, the chance to serve is often its own reward.

At times, to those who work in higher education, it seems as if the institution has forgotten, if it ever knew, that retired faculty and their families are potential contributors to the annual fund or capital fund of the institution. For many emeriti, a bequest to the institution that supported their lifelong pursuit of knowledge and teaching would be an appropriate and gracious act.

. . . emeritus faculty . . . are also often excellent ambassadors for the institution . . .

Some faculty see the chance to contribute as a way of returning something to the institution. Other faculty face the prospect of preparing a will without an appropriate heir and feel that the highest use of a bequest would be to their college. And there are always those few who have accumulated so much wealth that the institution in which they taught for so many years naturally becomes one of the objects of their beneficence. Though this is not a sufficient reason to treat emeritus as valuable members of the academy, it is an appropriate consideration.

Emeritus faculty, who are no longer regular university employees, could be employed on a part-time, ad hoc, or consultant basis when appropriate services are performed. Many emeriti may not need or want payment for what they do, but others might. Reimbursement for professional activities like travel to a professional meeting may be important to many emeritus faculty. In some cases, arrangements may be so made that there is little direct cost to the institution. In many cases, the principle of continuing meaningful association with the university for those who want it and have something to contribute is more important than the money involved.

The "Portable" Emeritus Status

If the benefits to both the institution and the faculty are clear, it does not seem to make a great deal of difference as to where the rank is held or whether it is carried to another college. One of the provosts interviewed in preparation for this report described the benefits to his college from recognizing emeritus faculty from other institutions. Usually these were distinguished faculty who moved to the area of his college and who desired a close working relationship with a nearby institution. As described by the provost, the informal relationships with emeriti worked very well. Some taught classes in areas or specialties in which the college found itself without full-time faculty; others worked with advanced students in specialized areas of a discipline or profession. Other emeritus faculty carried out important research, benefiting both colleagues and the students who helped them.

Institutional Planning for a New Emeritus Rank

There is little information at present on which to base generalizations about the roles emeritus faculty members are likely to have in the future. Therefore, institutional research might produce reliable and up-to-date information that could be particularly useful for planning purposes. A good place to start might be with several active emeritus or retired faculty and several interested employed faculty who command respect in the institution. Such a group, appointed by the college or by the faculty senate or jointly, could be charged with the responsibility of looking into the question and reporting back to the appointing authority.

Such a group might want to interview faculty and administrators, develop a survey, write to emeritus faculty associations at sister institutions, review the literature, and in general become familiar with local issues and possibilities.

The actual rights, privileges, obligations, and kind and degree of involvement of the emeritus professor in university affairs are quite inconsistent among institutions, and the criteria used to determine which retirees are awarded emeritus rank differ markedly among universities. Thus, understanding the differences and coming to some appropriate agreement as to the definition of emeritus and consistent criteria for awarding the rank are good places to start in planning.

For individual institutions, it seems important and timely to collect and analyze retirement and emeritus status data from institutional policies and practices, from the activities of faculty members, and on the current and future desires and intentions of both. Neither sound base-line data nor meaningful projections are available nationally now. The systematic gathering, examination, and reporting of such data at the institutional level would seem to be prudent and appropriate planning activities.

Tenure is being examined anew by some because the nature and length of permanent tenure will clearly be affected by the removal of the compulsory retirement age. Planning for the new emeritus rank would thus include ascertaining the number of tenured and nontenured faculty by age, race, sex, discipline, department, and projected retirement date. These data might then be compared with what is known about trends in student enrollments, institutional goals and emphases, which areas are to grow and expand, and which areas are to remain constant and perhaps decline. Planning for the future of the institution would seem to require some understanding of those numbers and their impact.

Further, planning for the new rank should take into consideration that intellectual and physical competence now extend, for many academic and professional men and women, beyond 62 or 65, common retirement ages previously established. In addition, the mandatory retirement option may now be closed; that makes planning for uncapping all the more important. Institutions can allow themselves to be placed at the mercy of events, or they can plan to exert some direction over those events.

As a result of such planning, institutions may alter their policies and practices so as to change the previous "emeritus professor" image from an honorific rank of distinguished faculty to one stressing productivity as well. For many professors, retirement will no longer mean withdrawal from active work at the prime of one's academic career but a transition to a new, less-pressure-filled life and professional role.

Albert (1986, p. 25) reminds us that "retirement terminates neither experience nor expertise . . . ." He also points out that allowing "this act of disengagement to mean a severing of all ties between an institution and an emeritus can only result in a measure of loss to both . . . ." In the future, institutions may plan ways for the option to be open to faculty to continue the scholarly work in all its various aspects but at a less hectic pace and under newly negotiated terms of employment.

It would seem prudent for the individual institution to plan, with faculty, the specific nature of privileges and responsibilities that will be expected of emeritus faculty. Many such privileges and responsibilities are likely to be found among the list of possible roles mentioned earlier. Many of these are privileges, and some faculty would even argue that they are or should be rights. However, it is likely that the future will be negotiated. Many of the items, as well as others, will be balanced in the sense that there will be both rights and responsibilities. What may start out as a list of demands that appear to benefit emeriti may end up as a carefully planned and agreed-upon role that is mutually beneficial.

Summary

Because of the high probability of total uncapping as of January 1, 1994, and the mounting of advocacy campaigns for retired and emeritus faculty, there is some sense of urgency for putting in place a new interpretation of the emeritus rank. The proposed emeritus rank would be academically the equal of full professor rank, but specific conditions of employment at emeritus rank would be negotiated. Cost-benefit ratios should be examined in open discussions with faculty so as to work out arrangements that are mutually satisfactory to both faculty and institutions. Emeritus faculty are likely to have a variety of roles and make a variety of contributions to higher education. Emeritus status should be portable from one institution to another and a new emeritus rank planned at the institutional level.

CONCLUSIONS AND RECOMMENDATIONS

This report was devoted to finding and to analyzing the professional literature on the emeritus professorship. It was anticipated that evidence might be found in the literature to suggest that significant changes were taking place in the meaning of emeritus status. Further, it was postulated that the emerging changes in the meaning of the emeritus rank could be used to help manage problems foreseen in connection with the impending demise of a mandatory retirement age for tenured faculty in higher education.

These expectations were based on a modest preliminary inspection of a sample of the literature. A fuller review and analysis showed the initial impression to be valid.

The literature proved to be widely dispersed and quite varied in content. Much of it was either highly personal and anecdotal or very speculative. There was, however, a core of research, consisting mainly of studies of how emeriti spent their time and studies about relationships they had or desired with their former employing colleges and universities. In addition, reports of the activities of emeriti organizations were located, and policy documents and bargaining agreements that recognized and described emeritus standing were found. To examine a possible relationship between emeritus status and retirement age, literature on the latter was incorporated in the review also.

Conclusions

Eight conclusions can be drawn from this study:

1. A body of literature on the emeritus professorship exists that is limited in scope but still large enough and substantive enough to warrant more attention than it now receives in the journals and texts.
2. There are applicable theories on which to build a broad body of knowledge on emeriti founded on rigorous, theory-based research. Such investigations could be of real value in making staffing plans and projections, at the same time adding to an understanding of an important and growing segment of the older population.
3. Emeritus faculty are in the process of building local, state, and national organizations. The faculty are motivated by enlightened self-interest and a desire for continued academic and professional engagement. Such organizations promise to become both large and powerful. They are

now at the stage where they could find homes on college or university campuses or find recognition, attachment, or alliances elsewhere.

4. Sufficient information and experience are reported in the literature on emeritus status to encourage the design and implementation of a new concept of emeritus professor as a part-time faculty rank incorporated into the traditional working rank structure of the professoriat.

5. Colleges and universities will have to find new ways to relate to older faculty while providing individual incentives for participating faculty members in keeping with institutional objectives. A promising way to do that is via the formalization of a working emeritus rank.

6. The time between now and 1994 constitutes a fortuitous window of opportunity in which to use the emeritus working rank as a means of cushioning the impact of uncapping. Yet the window is narrowing day by day.

7. It is often noted in discussions on retirement age and retirement intentions that average age of faculty retirement is now markedly below age 70 and is falling. According to literature now available, such an assumption may be open to question in some types of institutions. Moreover, average retirement age may be less relevant than the mounting evidence that larger proportions and numbers of faculty intend to continue working beyond age 70.

8. Far too few institutions of higher education have sufficient information about faculty retirement intentions, either before or after uncapping, to make projections for local use or to determine state, regional, or national trends. That seems to be the case for all types of institutions. Large-scale studies with the prospect of correcting that condition are only now getting under way.

These eight conclusions are the major outcomes of the available literature. The next section deals with recommendations, most of which have their roots in the above conclusions. It must be concluded from the literature now available that such a discussion is needed and essential.

Recommendations
We recommend that institutions come to agreement as to the definition of emeritus and determine fair and consistent criteria for awarding it.

Individual institutions will find it necessary to collect and analyze retirement and emeritus status data from institutional policies and practices, the activities of faculty members, and the current and future desires and intentions of both.

Institutions should alter their policies and practices so as to change the previous "emeritus professor" image from a rank of retired faculty to a new form of working rank, part time, equally distinguished, but accenting productivity as well. For many professors, retirement will no longer mean withdrawal from active work at the prime of one's academic career but a transition to a new, less hectic life and professional role in the new emeritus rank. Colleges and universities should enable older scholars to retire and to remain active in retirement by offering a working emeritus rank for those who want to remain active and productive but at a more relaxed pace.

Our recommendation is that institutions put real meaning and distinction into the emeritus rank and reserve it for the most active and interested faculty. Faculty then might be more likely to treat the rank as a meaningful opportunity to make additional contributions rather than as an honorific title without meaningful responsibilities or challenges.

Among the enticements that could be recommended are office and laboratory space, secretarial help, library and parking privileges, part- or full-time graduate assistance, computer or laboratory facilities, and opportunities to teach, carry on research, and work with students part time. One of the biggest fears faculty have about retirement is that they will be cut off from colleagues and students and the rich intellectual environment they are used to, and some such arrangement would allay that fear of retirement.

We also recommend this new rank of emeritus faculty be portable in appropriate circumstances. The benefits to one college from recognizing emeritus faculty from other institutions might be quite substantial. Distinguished faculty who move to another area where there are institutions of higher education could continue their contributions.

We also recommend that individual institutions examine the roles emeritus faculty members are likely to have in the future. The research each institution conducts might produce reliable and up-to-date information that could be useful for planning purposes.

Each institution should work to involve active emeritus or retired faculty as well as currently employed faculty who command respect in the institution in the development of policies governing emeritus faculty. They could interview faculty and administrators, develop a questionnaire, write to emeritus faculty associations at sister institutions, review the literature, including this book, and in general become familiar with policies and issues locally.

Each institution, with faculty, should search for ways to acknowledge voluntary emeritus faculty contributions in scholarship, research, teaching, and service. The new relationship suggested here between institutions and emeritus faculty should be, if it is to be viable and lasting, mutually beneficial; ideally both should gain.

There should be social and economic benefits to the new relationship if it is to remain healthy. Certainly, some emeritus faculty feel so loyal to their schools that they may not wish to seek financial compensation for teaching, advising, consultation, or other academic and professional contributions. And no doubt there are institutions that do not want to ask emeritus faculty to contribute their skills when there is little possibility of adequate pay. There are several options that might be recommended, most of which could result in dividends for both the institution and the emeritus faculty member. For example, the faculty member could be compensated financially, then could make a gift in the amount of the compensation to the institution. The emeritus faculty then enjoys the pleasure and prestige of recognition as a contributor to the institutional mission. The college or university can announce another faculty contribution and take advantage of the known encouragement that gives to other potential contributors.

Those faculty who wish to continue in an active, productive relationship with the institution should be given space and support as appropriate. That form of recognition is usually highly prized by faculty members, yet it is relatively inexpensive when compared to a tenured faculty member's alternative of continued employment.

Highly recommended are the establishment and presentation of awards exclusively for extraordinary, otherwise uncompensated contributions in scholarship, teaching, research, or service by emeritus faculty. These represent only three of many possible ways to acknowledge the contributions of emeriti.

Colleges and universities must find ways to keep faculty active in retirement, whether the motivation is to retire some or to retain the services of some they would rather not lose. Emeritus associations that provide benefits on campus as well as organize social and academic events, lectures, workshops, seminars, and so forth, should be encouraged and supported in order to keep faculty active.

Colleges and universities must address the issue of a fair and equitable system of evaluation for tenured faculty, worked out with faculty and acceptable to both faculty and the administration.

Each institution needs to examine the possibility of a faculty shortage. It is by no means clear that there will be enough well-qualified faculty in some disciplines or professional areas to supply higher education in the future. Some evidence from the United States as well as abroad indicates that the future supply of higher education faculty may be scarce, not abundant. If this is true, good data and planning may help to assure a steady and appropriate supply of high-quality faculty.

We recommend that each institution obtain its own information in anticipation of uncapping, as well as keep up with new studies being done, such as the congressionally mandated study by the National Academy of Sciences. Within each institution, it may be time to study both the past retirement behavior and the future retirement intentions of faculty by categories, such as age, sex, race, academic discipline, and academic preparation.

Issues for Further Study
Several matters require further study:

1. The definition of emeritus and criteria common to its awarding in institutions of higher education.
2. The intentions of those faculty who are nearing the age of retirement but who will not be required to retire.
3. The knowledge and understanding of faculty in general about the meaning and implications for them in the ADEA.
4. A cost-benefit analysis of the effects of different retirement policies in operation presently in institutions without mandatory retirement ages for faculty.
5. Case studies of institutions that have criteria for a meaningful rank of emeritus faculty to determine the results.
6. An analysis of the emeritus perquisites that would lead faculty to retire, including the attractiveness of each one with various categories of faculty.

7. Successful models of faculty development and evaluation throughout the career of tenured faculty.
8. An analysis of the costs and benefits of present early retirement programs.

Summary

What once seemed a natural linkage—tenure and a retirement age of 65 coupled with the beginning of pension benefits—has come apart. There no longer is a "normal" date or age for retirement, and there appears to be no easy way to reanchor the termination of employment temporally or financially. Instead, it appears that individual rather than arbitrary solutions must be attempted. One solution with considerable promise is individually negotiated, phased retirement, with tenure, making use of a transfer to a redefined emeritus rank.

It can be expected that there will soon be strong, active organizations of emeritus faculty at the campus, state, regional, national, and, possibly, international levels. It is too early to predict what the emeritus organizations' ties might be to other professional organizations and to organizations of retired persons in general. It does seem certain, however, that there could be competition for affiliation with emeritus groups because of the quality, variety, vigor, and prestige of the persons making up the emeritus groups.

The studies reported to date offer conflicting answers to whether uncapping will result in delaying the average age of retirement. Other powerful forces are at work—the aging faculty, supply and demand, inflation, and structural changes in society.

REFERENCES

The Educational Resources Information Center (ERIC) Clearinghouse on Higher Education abstracts and indexes the current literature on higher education for inclusion in ERIC's data base and announcement in ERIC's monthly bibliographic journal, *Resources in Education* (RIE). Most of these publications are available through the ERIC Document Reproduction Service (EDRS). For publications cited in this bibliography that are available from EDRS, ordering number and price code are included. Readers who wish to order a publication should write to the ERIC Document Reproduction Service, 3900 Wheeler Avenue, Alexandria, Virginia 22304. (Phone orders with VISA or MasterCard are taken at 800/227-ERIC or 703/823-0500.) When ordering, please specify the document (ED) number. Documents are available as noted in microfiche (MF) and paper copy (PC). If you have the price code ready when you call EDRS, an exact price can be quoted. The last page of the latest issue of *Resources in Education* also has the current cost, listed by code.

AAUP. 1940. "Statement of Principles on Academic Freedom and Tenure." Washington, D.C.: American Association of University Professors.

————. September/October 1982. "Uncapping the Mandatory Retirement Age." *Academe* 68: 14a–18a.

————. 1983a. "Agreement between Bloomfield College and the Bloomfield College Chapter of the American Association of University Professors and Bloomfield College Faculty Personnel Procedures. July 1, 1983, to June 30, 1985." ED 257 367. 41 pp. MF–01; PC–02.

————. 1983b. "Agreement between Wilberforce University and the Wilberforce University Faculty Association, Effective September 26, 1983, through August 31, 1986." ED 257 410. 38 pp. MF–01; PC–02.

————. 1984. "Agreement between the Board of Trustees of Union County College and the Union County College Chapter of the AAUP. September 1, 1984, to August 31, 1987." ED 257 406. 111 pp. MF–01; PC–05.

————. 1987a. "Agreement between Utica College of Syracuse University and American Association of University Professors, Utica College Chapter. Expires August 31, 1987." ED 257 407. 41 pp. MF–01; PC–02.

————. July/August 1987b. "Working Paper on the Status of Tenure without Mandatory Retirement." *Academe* 73: 45–48.

————. January/February 1988. "Statement of Principles on Academic Retirement and Insurance Plans." *Academe* 74: 37–38.

Albert, Sydney P. July/August 1986. "Retirement: From Rite to Rights." *Academe* 72: 24–26.

Appley, A.H. 1987. "The Academic Retiree: Recycling Wisdom."

Academy Notes 6: 4–6.

Auerbach, A.J. 1986a. "The Emeritus College: Boon or Boondoggle?" Paper presented at the annual meeting of the Association of Gerontology in Higher Education, February 28, Atlanta, Georgia. ED 268 916. 7 pp. MF–01; PC–01.

———. 1986b. "Emeritus Professors: Engagement and Involvement." *Educational Gerontology* 10: 277–87.

———. Fall 1986c. "Professors in Retirement: The Emeritus College Model." *College Board Review* No. 141: 22–36.

Baldwin, Roger. September 1984. "The Changing Development Needs of an Aging Professorate." New Directions for Teaching and Learning No. 19. San Francisco: Jossey-Bass.

Benjamin, Ernst. Spring 1988. "Pensions, Retirement, and Tenure: What Can Faculty Expect in the Future?" In *Footnotes.* Washington, D.C.: American Association of University Professors.

Benz, M. 1958. "A Study of Faculty and Administrative Staff Who Have Retired from New York University." *Journal of Educational Sociology* 31: 282–93.

Bertelsen, Katherine Huggins. 1983. "Phased Retirement: A Way to Enhance Quality." Paper read at an annual meeting of the Southern Regional Council on Educational Administration, November 13–15, Knoxville, Tennessee. ED 247 652. 39 pp. MF–01; PC–02.

Blackburn, J.O., and S. Schiffmann. 1980. "Faculty Retirement at the COFHE Institutions: An Analysis of the Impact of Age 70 Mandatory Retirement and Options for Institutional Response." Cambridge, Mass.: Consortium on Financing Higher Education. ED 233 643. 90 pp. MF–01; PC–04.

Blum, Debra E. 26 October 1988. "UCLA's Emeriti Association Shows 'There Is Life beyond Retirement.'" *Chronicle of Higher Education:* A16–A17.

———. 15 February 1989a. "Ban on Mandatory Retirement Age Not Likely to Affect Most Professors' Retirement Plans, Survey Finds." *Chronicle of Higher Education.*

———. 3 May 1989b. "Bargaining Is Stalled among Professors, Study Center Says." *Chronicle of Higher Education.*

Bowen, Howard R., and Jack H. Schuster. 1986. *American Professors.* New York: Oxford Univ. Press.

Bowen, William G., and Julie Ann Sosa. 1989. *Prospects for Faculty in the Arts and Sciences: A Study of Factors Affecting Demand and Supply, 1987–2012.* Princeton, N.J.: Princeton Univ. Press.

Brown, R.S. July/August 1988. "1988 Report of the Council Committee on Retirement." *Academe* 74: 34–35.

Burkhauser, Richard V., and Joseph F. Quinn. 1989. "An Economy-Wide View of Changing Mandatory Retirement Rules." In *Mandatory Retirement: Effects on Higher Education,* edited by Karen C. Holden and W. Lee Hansen. New Directions for Higher Education No. 65. San Francisco: Jossey-Bass.

Calvin, Allen. 1984. "Age Discrimination on Campus." AAHE *Bulletin* 37(3): 1–7. ED 250 999. 6 pp. MF–01; PC–01.

Chronister, J.L., and T.R. Kepple, Jr. 1987. *Incentive Early Retirement Programs for Faculty: Innovative Responses to a Changing Environment.* ASHE-ERIC Higher Education Report No. 1. Washington, D.C.: Association for the Study of Higher Education. ED 283 478. 98 pp. MF–01; PC–04.

Chronister, J.L., and A. Trainer. 1985. "Early, Partial, and Phased Retirement Programs in Public Higher Education." *Journal of the College and University Personal Association* 36: 27–31.

Ciardi, John. 1980. *A Browser's Dictionary.* New York: Harper & Row.

Clark, Shirley M., and Darrell R. Lewis, eds. 1985. *Faculty Vitality and Institutional Productivity: Critical Perspectives for Higher Education.* New York: Teachers College Press.

COFHE. 1989. "Faculty Benefit Retirement Study: 1988." Cambridge, Mass.: Consortium on Financing Higher Education.

Committee A on Academic Freedom and Tenure. July/August 1987. "Working Paper on the Status of Tenure without Mandatory Retirement." *Academe* 73: 45–48.

Committee on Aging. 1986. *The Removal of Age Ceiling Cap under the Age Discrimination in Employment Act.* Joint hearing before the Subcommittee on Employment Opportunities of the Committee on Education and Labor and the Subcommittee on Health and Long-Term Care of the Select Committee on Aging. House of Representatives, 99th Congress, 2d Session. Washington, D.C.: U.S. Government Printing Office. ED 271 704. 125 pp. MF–01; PC–05.

Corwin, Thomas M., and Paula R. Knepper. 1978. "Finance and Employment Implications of Raising the Mandatory Retirement Age for Faculty." *Policy Analysis Service* 4(1). Washington, D.C.: American Council on Education. ED 163 868. 72 pp. MF–01; PC–03.

Covert-McGrath, Debra. 1984. "NACUBO Report: Early and Phased Retirement." Washington, D.C.: National Association of College and University Business Officers. ED 246 743. 7 pp. MF–01; PC–01.

Cronk, L. May/June 1989. "Strings Attached." *The Sciences* 2: 4.

Cummings, E., L. Dean, D.S. Newell, and I. McCaffrey. 1960. "Disengagements: A Tentative Theory of Aging." *Sociometry* 23: 23–25.

Dillard, John. 1982. "Life Satisfaction of Nearly Retired and Retired Workers." *Journal of Employment Counseling* 19: 131–34.

Dooris, Michael J., and G. Gregory Lozier. 1987. "The Graying of Faculty: Challenges and Opportunities." Presentation to the Society for College and University Planning, July 21.

Dorfman, Lorraine T. 1978. "Professors in Retirement: A Study of the Activities and Reactions to Retirement of University of Iowa Emeritus Faculty." Ph.D. dissertation, Univ. of Iowa.

———. 1980. "Emeritus Professors: Correlates of Professional Activity in Retirement." *Research in Higher Education* 12: 301–16.

———. 1981. "Emeritus Professors: Correlates of Professional Activity in Retirement II." *Research in Higher Education* 14: 147–60.

———. 1982. "Retired Professors and Professional Activity: A Comparative Study of Three Types of Institutions." *Research in Higher Education* 17: 249–66.

———. 1984. "Reactions of Professors to Retirement: A Comparison of Retired Faculty from Three Types of Institutions." *Research in Higher Education* 20: 89–102.

———. 1985. "Retired Academics and Professional Activity: A British-American Comparison." *Research in Higher Education* 22: 273–89.

Finkin, Matthew W. 1988. "Commentary: Tenure after an Uncapped ADEA: A Different View." *Journal of College and University Law* 15: 43–61.

———. 1989. "Tenure after the ADEA Amendments: A Different View." In *Mandatory Retirement: Effects on Higher Education,* edited by Karen C. Holden and W. Lee Hansen. New Directions for Higher Education No. 65. San Francisco: Jossey-Bass.

Gray, Kevin. 1989. *Retirement Plans and Expectations of TIAA-CREF Policy Holders.* New York: Teachers Insurance and Annuity Association/College Retirement Equities Fund.

Habecker, Eugene B. 1981. *A Systematic Approach to the Study of Benefits and Determinants of Tenure in American Higher Education: An Analysis of the Evidence.* ED 212 208. 66 pp. MF–01; PC–03.

Hansen, Bernard L. 1985. "Election of Early Retirement and Other Flexibility Options by Ontario Faculty: Past, Present, and Future." In *The Professoriate: Occupation in Crisis,* edited by Cecely Watson. Toronto: Ontario Institute for Studies in Education. ED 265 816. 396 pp. MF–01; PC–16.

Hansen, W. Lee. 1985. "Changing Demography of Faculty in Higher Education." In *Faculty Vitality and Institutional Productivity,* edited by Shirley M. Clark and Darrell R. Lewis. New York: Teachers College Press.

Havighurst, Robert J. 1985. "Aging and Productivity: The Case of Older Faculty." In *Faculty Vitality and Institutional Productivity,* edited by Shirley M. Clark and Darrell R. Lewis. New York: Teachers College Press.

Heller, Scott. 1986. "Colleges Ponder the Effects on Tenure of End to Mandatory Retirement at 70." *Chronicle of Higher Education* 33: 15+.

Hellweg, Susan, and Davis A. Churchman. Fall 1981. "The Academic Tenure System: Unplanned Obsolescence in an Era of Retrenchment." *Planning for Higher Education* 10: 16–18.

Holden, Karen C. 1985. "Maintaining Faculty Vitality through Early Retirement Options." In *Faculty Vitality and Institutional Productivity,* edited by Shirley M. Clark and Darrell R. Lewis. New York: Teachers College Press.

Holden, Karen C., and W. Lee Hansen. 1989a. "Eliminating Mandatory Retirement: Effects on Retirement Age." In *The End of Mandatory Retirement: Effects on Higher Education,* edited by Karen C. Holden and W. Lee Hansen. San Francisco: Jossey-Bass.

———. 1989b. "Retirement Behavior and Mandatory Retirement in Higher Education." In *The End of Mandatory Retirement: Effects on Higher Education,* edited by Karen C. Holden and W. Lee Hansen. San Francisco: Jossey-Bass.

———, eds. 1989c. *The End of Mandatory Retirement: Effects on Higher Education.* San Francisco: Jossey-Bass.

Institute for Research in Social Behavior. 1980. *Retirement Plans and Related Factors among Faculty at COFHE Institutions.* Cambridge, Mass.: Consortium on Financing Higher Education. ED 233 645. 217 pp. MF–01; PC–09.

Jennings, S. March 1988. "NEA Part-time Faculty Report Issued at Higher Education Meeting." *Higher Education Advocate* 5: 1–2.

Johnson, Diane. 1983. "The Academy of Independent Scholars: An Intellectual Resource of 'Proven Creativity.'" *Change* 15: 41–43.

Kellams, Samuel, and Jay L. Chronister. 1988. "Life after Early Retirement: Faculty Activities and Perceptions." Occasional Paper Series. Charlottesville, Va.: Center for the Study of Higher Education.

Lee, Barbara A. 1989. "Academic Personnel Policies and Practices: Managing the Process." In *Managing Faculty Resources,* edited by G. Gregory Lozier and Michael J. Dooris. New Directions for Institutional Research. San Francisco: Jossey-Bass.

Licata, Christine M. 1986. *Post-tenure Faculty Evaluation: Threat or Opportunity?* ASHE-ERIC Higher Education Report No. 1. Washington, D.C.: Association for the Study of Higher Education. ED 270 009. 118 pp. MF–01; PC–05.

Lozier, G. Gregory, and Michael J. Dooris. 1987. "Is Higher Education Confronting Faculty Shortages?" Paper read at an annual meeting of the Association for the Study of Higher Education, November 21–24, Baltimore, Maryland. ED 292 386. 20 pp. MF–01; PC–01.

———. 1988–89. "Elimination of Mandatory Retirement: Anticipating Faculty Response." *Planning for Higher Education* 17: 1–14.

———, eds. 1989. *Managing Faculty Resources.* New Directions for Institutional Research. San Francisco: Jossey-Bass.

McDonagh, Edward C. 1987. "A Comparison of Benefits and Perquisites of Emeriti Faculty at Ohio State University with a Sample of

74 Land-Grant Colleges and/or Members of the National Association of State Universities." Mimeographed. Columbus: Ohio State University.

Mangan, Katherine S. 26 October 1988. "Colleges Offering Added Benefits to Retired Professors in Effort to Make Quitting Appeal to Older Scholars." *Chronicle of Higher Education.*

Mauch, James, Jack W. Birch, and Jack Matthews. 1989a. "Emeritus Rank in Major Research Universities." Pittsburgh: Univ. of Pittsburgh.

————. 1989b. "Emeritus Status in Pennsylvania Colleges and Universities." Pittsburgh: Univ. of Pittsburgh.

Miller, Richard I. 1987. *Evaluating Faculty for Promotion and Tenure.* San Francisco: Jossey-Bass.

Milletti, Mario A. 1984. *Voices of Experience: 1,500 Retired People Talk about Retirement.* New York: TIAA-CREF, Educational Research. ED 249 844. 201 pp. MF–01; PC–09.

Mirel, Lawrence H. 1977. "Emeritus Status: Alternative to Retirement." *Worklife* 2: 7–10.

Mitchel, Barbara A. 1981. "Early Retirement in Higher Education." Paper presented at an annual meeting of the Association for the Study of Higher Education, March, Washington, D.C. ED 203 802. 16 pp. MF–01; PC–01.

Monahan, Deborah J. 1987. "Predictors of Early Retirement among University Faculty." *Gerontologist* 27: 46–52.

Montgomery, Sarah. 1989. "Findings from the COFHE Studies." In *Mandatory Retirement: Effects on Higher Education,* edited by Karen C. Holden and W. Lee Hansen. New Directions for Higher Education No. 65. San Francisco: Jossey-Bass.

Mooney, Carolyn J. 1987. "Expected End of Mandatory Retirement in 1990s Unlikely to Cause Glut of Professors, Study Finds." *Chronicle of Higher Education* 34: 1.

Mortimer, K.P., M. Bagshaw, and A. Masland. 1985. *Flexibility in Academic Staffing: Effective Policies and Practices.* ASHE-ERIC Higher Education Report No. 1. Washington, D.C.: Association for the Study of Higher Education. ED 260 675. 121 pp. MF–01; PC–05.

Mulanaphy, James M. 1981. *Plans and Expectations for Retirement of TIAA-CREF Participants.* New York: Teachers Insurance and Annuity Association. ED 208 785. 78 pp. MF–01; PC–04.

Myers, Betty Jane, and Richard E. Pearson. 1984. "Personal Perspective of Academic Professionals Approaching Retirement." New Directions for Teaching and Learning No. 19. San Francisco: Jossey-Bass.

Over, Ray. September 1982. "Does Research Productivity Decline with Age?" *Higher Education* 7: 511–20.

Peterson, James A., Arnold M. Small, and John Schneider. n.d. "Survey of Retired Faculty and Staff Organizations of Universities and Colleges in the USA." Mimeographed. Los Angeles: Univ. of Southern California.

Pifer, Alan, and D. Lydia Bronte, eds. 1986. *Our Aging Society: A Challenge for the Future*. New York: W.W. Norton.

Pratt, Henry J. 1989. "Uncapping Mandatory Retirement: The Lobbyists' Influence." In *Mandatory Retirement: Effects on Higher Education,* edited by Karen C. Holden and W. Lee Hansen. New Directions for Higher Education No. 65. San Francisco: Jossey-Bass.

Prochaska, Patricia. 1987. *Age Discrimination in Employment: Current Legal Developments*. CRS Report for Congress. Washington, D.C.: Library of Congress.

Reskin, Barbara F. 1985. "Aging and Productivity: Career and Results." In *Faculty Vitality and Institutional Productivity,* edited by Shirley M. Clark and Darrell R. Lewis. New York: Teachers College Press.

Riley, Matilda White. July/August 1986. "On Future Demands for Older Professors." *Academe* 72: 14–16.

Roe, A. 1965. "Changes in Scientific Activities with Age." *Science* 150: 313–18.

Roman, P., and P. Taietz. 1967. "Organizational Structure and Disengagement: The Emeritus Professor." *Gerontologist* 7: 147–52.

Rose, A.M. 1965. "A Current Sociological Issue in Gerontology." In *Older People and Their Social World,* edited by A.M. Rose and W.A. Peterson. Philadelphia: F.A. Davis.

Rowe, Alan R. 1976. "Retired Academics and Research Activity." *Journal of Gerontology* 31: 456–60.

Ruebhausen, Oscar M. 1988. "The Age Discrimination in Employment Act Amendments of 1986: Implications for Tenure and Retirement." *Journal of College and University Law* 14: 561–74.

–––––––. 1989. "Implications of the 1986 ADEA Amendments for Tenure and Retirement." In *Mandatory Retirement: Effects on Higher Education,* edited by Karen C. Holden and W. Lee Hansen. New Directions for Higher Education No. 65. San Francisco: Jossey-Bass.

Ruebhausen, Oscar M., and Thomas C. Woodruff. July/August 1986. "Retirement Programs for College and University Personnel." *Academe* 72: 8–13.

Sharon, Jared B. 1979. "Learning from Here to Eternity." New Directions for Community Colleges No. 7. San Francisco: Jossey-Bass.

Soldofsky, Robert M. 1984. "Age and Productivity of University Faculties: A Case Study." *Economics of Education Review* 3: 289–98.

–––––––. July/August 1986. "On Determining the Optimal Retirement Age." *Academe* 72: 17–23.

Stuen, Cynthia, and Lenard W. Kaye. Fall 1984. "Creating Educational Alliances between Retired Academics, Community Agencies, and Elderly Neighborhood Residents." *Community Services Catalyst* 14: 21–24.

Sumberg, Alfred D. 1989. "Tax Changes, Retirement, and Pensions." In *Mandatory Retirement: Effects on Higher Education,* edited by Karen C. Holden and W. Lee Hansen. New Directions for Higher Education No. 65. San Francisco: Jossey-Bass.

TIAA-CREF. October 1988a. "Group Health Insurance Coverage of Retired Employees." Research Dialogues No. 10. New York: Teachers Insurance and Annuity Association/College Retirement Equities Fund.

————. July 1988b. "Voluntary Incentive Early Retirement Programs." Research Dialogues No. 16. New York: Teachers Insurance and Annuity Association/College Retirement Equities Fund.

Trice, Mildred Moore. 1981. "Life Styles of Retired Professors." Ph.D. dissertation, Univ. of Pittsburgh.

U.S. Department of Labor. 1982. *Final Report to Congress on Age Discrimination in Employment Act Studies.* Washington, D.C.: U.S. Government Printing Office.

Walker, George H., Jr. 1972. "Status of Phased Retirement in Higher Education." Mount Pleasant: Central Michigan Univ. ED 054 752. 8 pp. MF-01; PC-01.

Weiler, William C. Winter 1989. "Abolition of Mandatory Retirement." *Educational Record:* 59–62.

Ycas, Martynas A. 1987. "Recent Trends in Health Near the Age of Retirement: New Findings from the Health Interview Survey." *Social Security Bulletin* 50(2).

INDEX

A

AAU (see Association of American Universities)
AAUP (see American Association of University Professors)
   Academic rank, 5
ADEA (see Age Discrimination in Employment Act)
Advocacy, 15
Age criterion
       retirement, 3
Age discrimination, 7
       state laws, 8
Age Discrimination in Employment Act, 6
Aging
       realities, 22
Aging population, 23
Air traffic controllers, 7
Airline pilots, 7
Alfred P. Sloan Foundation, 39
American Association of University Professors (AAUP), 3, 32, 39, 46
       Executive Committee, 49
       "Statement of Principles on Academic Retirement and
          Insurance Plans", 49
American Council on Education, 27
American Federation of Teachers, 27
Association of American Universities (AAU), 5, 40
Average retirement age, 19

B

Beloit College, 2
Bloomfield College, 47
Brown, Ralph S., 1

C

California Conference of AAUP, 32
California Faculty Association, 29
California State University system, 29
Canadian faculty, 30
Central Intelligence Agency, 7
Central State University, 47
Chronicle of Higher Education, 27
Collective bargaining contracts, 46
Collective bargaining, 34
Committee on Aging, 3, 23
Committee on Mandatory Retirement in Higher Education, 39
Compulsory retirement, 1, 40
Compulsory retirement age, 3, 41
Conclusions, 63, 64
Congress, 39

Consortium on Financing Higher Education, 19, 41
Cornell University, 16
Cost-benefit analysis, 54
Craig, Gordon A., 2
Crescitelli, Frederick N., 2

D

Deadwood, 12
Disengagement
    aging, 15, 16
Distinguished service, 42

E

Early retirement policies
    higher education institutions, 10
Early retirements, 9
Eckerd College, 29
Emeritus and Retired Faculty Association, 29
Emeritus College, 29
Emeritus faculty
    as resources, 57
    changing roles, 34
    future roles, 55
    reemployment, 43
Emeritus faculty organizations, 53
Emeritus faculty role, 28
Emeritus policies
    surveys, 40
Emeritus professor
    activity, 1, 2
    definition, 4
    meaning, 3, 4
    obligations, 3
    privileges, 3
    rights, 3
Emeritus professorship
    bona fide rank, 36
    criteria, 2
Emeritus rank
    institutional planning, 58-60
    new interpretation, 9, 53
    new meaning, 13
    relationship with existing ranks, 53
Emeritus rights, 32, 33
    faculty privileges, 32
    financial counseling, 32
    preretirement information, 32

Emeritus status
  and uncapping, 35
  appointment criteria, 42
  collective bargaining, 34
  criteria, 42
  definition, 32
  institutions awarding, 41-48
  issues for further study, 67
  portability, 58
  privileges, 42, 44
  professional lifestyle, 31
  review, 3
  views of faculty, 30, 31
Employment
  higher education, 3, 8
Employment Act of 1946, 6
Equal Employment Opportunity Commission, 12
ERIC, 46

F

Faculty personnel policies, 1
Faculty privileges, 42
Faculty requirements and wishes, 10
Faculty retirement
  ages, 26
Fair Labor Standards Act Amendments
  exemptions, 7
Ford Foundation, 2

G

Gerontological grouping, 24
Gomory, Ralph E., 39
Group health plans, 7

H

Health and intellect, 23
Higher education
  dilemmas, 9
  faculty structure, 26
  financing, 26
Higher education groups, 14
Higher education institutions, 8

I

Incentives
  early retirement, 9

J

James, Thomas W., 2

K

Key terms
 definition, 5

L

Labor market participation, 18
Life span and economic implications, 22
Lozier-Dooris study, 41

M

Mandatory retirement age, 1, 5
Medical benefits, 25
Medicare, 7
Medieval professors, 6
Meritorious teachers and researchers, 35
Middle Ages, 6

N

National Academy of Sciences, 39
National Education Association (NEA), 27, 46
New emeriti, 1
New York University, 16
Northern Michigan University
 retirees association, 48

O

Ohio State University Retirees Association, 29
Older Americans Act of 1965, 6
Older faculty
 needs, 9
Older persons
 differences among, 24
Older scholars and institutions
 interaction, 17
Ontario Canada, 30
Oxford American Dictionary, 4

P

Pennsylvania, 40, 41
Pension plans, 5, 25
"Portable" emeritus status, 58
Princeton University, 39
Private support, 11
Productive faculty members, 10, 15, 36
Project on Faculty Retirement, 39

Promotion and tenure mechanisms, 12
Public support, 11

R

Recommendations
       emeritus status, 64-67
Rees, Albert, 39
Replacement faculty, 11
Retired faculty
       continuing roles, 28, 29
Retirement
       alternative definitions, 1
       economic factors, 25
Retirement age uncapping, 17
Retirement status
       definition, 32
Retiring personnel
       replacement, 20
Role continuity of faculty, 15, 16, 36
Roles of emeriti, 56

S

Salary budgets, 11
Services and facilities, 42
Smith, Sharon P., 39
Social Security Administration, 18
Southern Illinois University, 29
Stages of aging, 24
Stanford University, 2
State law
       age discrimination, 8
Surplus faculty
       reassignment, 20

T

Tax Reform Act of 1986, 25
Tax-deferred compensation, 26
Tenure, 6
       termination, 12
Tenure disputes, 12
Tenure revision, 49
       and uncapping, 49
Tenure violation, 49
Tenured faculty, 5
       demographics, 39
TIAA-CREF, 19, 20, 27

U

UCLA, 2, 29
Uncapping, 35
    data, 17-20
    faculty understanding, 27
    tenure revision, 49
Union County College, 46
University of Massachusetts, 29
University of Pittsburgh Senate, 40
University of Southern California, 29
University of Washington, 29
U.S. Department of Labor, 17
U.S. Supreme Court, 12
Utica College, 47

W

Western Conference on Retirement in Colleges and
    Universities, 29
Wilberforce University, 47
Woodard, Henry G., 2
Working faculty, 45

Y

Yale University, 1

ASHE-ERIC HIGHER EDUCATION REPORTS

Since 1983, the Association for the Study of Higher Education (ASHE) and the Educational Resources Information Center (ERIC) Clearinghouse on Higher Education, a sponsored project of the School of Education and Human Development at The George Washington University, have cosponsored the *ASHE-ERIC Higher Education Report* series. The 1990 series is the nineteenth overall and the second to be published by the School of Education and Human Development at the George Washington University.

Each monograph is the definitive analysis of a tough higher education problem, based on thorough research of pertinent literature and insitutional experiences. Topics are identified by a national survey. Noted practitioners and scholars are then commissioned to write the reports, with experts providing critical reviews of each manuscript before publication.

Eight monographs (10 before 1985) in the ASHE-ERIC Higher Education Report series are published each year and are available on individual and subscription basis. Subscription to eight issues is $80.00 annually; $60 to members of AAHE, AIR, or AERA; and $50 to ASHE members. All foreign subscribers must include an additional $10 per series year for postage.

To order single copies of existing reports, use the order form on the last page of this book. Regular prices, and special rates available to members of AAHE, AIR, AERA and ASHE, are as follows:

Series	Regular	Members
1990	$17.00	$12.75
1988-89	15.00	11.25
1985-87	10.00	7.50
1983-84	7.50	6.00
before 1983	6.50	5.00

Price includes book rate postage within the U.S. For foreign orders, please add $1.00 per book. Fast United Parcel Service available within the U.S. at $2.50 for each order under $50.00, and calculated at 5% of invoice total for orders $50.00 or above.

All orders under $45.00 must be prepaid. Make check payable to ASHE-ERIC. For Visa or MasterCard, include card number, expiration date and signature. A bulk discount of 10% is available on orders of 15 or more books (not applicable on subscriptions).

Address order to
   ASHE-ERIC Higher Education Reports
   The George Washington University
   1 Dupont Circle, Suite 630
   Washington, DC 20036
Or phone (202) 296-2597
   Write for a complete catalog of ASHE-ERIC Higher Education Reports.

1990 ASHE-ERIC Higher Education Reports

1. The Campus Green: Fund Raising in Higher Education
   Barbara E. Brittingham and Thomas R. Pezzullo

1989 ASHE-ERIC Higher Education Reports

1. Making Sense of Administrative Leadership: The 'L' Word in
   Higher Education
   Estela M. Bensimon, Anna Neumann, and Robert Birnbaum

2. Affirmative Rhetoric, Negative Action: African-American and
   Hispanic Faculty at Predominantly White Universities
   Valora Washington and William Harvey

3. Postsecondary Developmental Programs: A Traditional Agenda
   with New Imperatives
   Louise M. Tomlinson

4. The Old College Try: Balancing Athletics and Academics in
   Higher Education
   John R. Thelin and Lawrence L. Wiseman

5. The Challenge of Diversity: Involvement or Alienation in the
   Academy?
   Daryl G. Smith

6. Student Goals for College and Courses: A Missing Link in Assessing and Improving Academic Achievement
   Joan S. Stark, Kathleen M. Shaw, and Malcolm A. Lowther

7. The Student as Commuter: Developing a Comprehensive Institutional Response
   Barbara Jacoby

8. Renewing Civic Capacity: Preparing College Students for Service
   and Citizenship
   Suzanne W. Morse

1988 ASHE-ERIC Higher Education Reports

1. The Invisible Tapestry: Culture in American Colleges and
   Universities
   George D. Kuh and Elizabeth J. Whitt

2. Critical Thinking: Theory, Research, Practice, and Possibilities
   Joanne Gainen Kurfiss

3. Developing Academic Programs: The Climate for Innovation
   Daniel T. Seymour

4. Peer Teaching: To Teach is To Learn Twice
   Neal A. Whitman

5. Higher Education and State Governments: Renewed Partnership,
   Cooperation, or Competition?
   Edward R. Hines

6. Entrepreneurship and Higher Education: Lessons for Colleges, Universities, and Industry
   James S. Fairweather

7. Planning for Microcomputers in Higher Education: Strategies for the Next Generation
   Reynolds Ferrante, John Hayman, Mary Susan Carlson, and Harry Phillips

8. The Challenge for Research in Higher Education: Harmonizing Excellence and Utility
   Alan W. Lindsay and Ruth T. Neumann

1987 ASHE-ERIC Higher Education Reports

1. Incentive Early Retirement Programs for Faculty: Innovative Responses to a Changing Environment
   Jay L. Chronister and Thomas R. Kepple, Jr.

2. Working Effectively with Trustees: Building Cooperative Campus Leadership
   Barbara E. Taylor

3. Formal Recognition of Employer-Sponsored Instruction: Conflict and Collegiality in Postsecondary Education
   Nancy S. Nash and Elizabeth M. Hawthorne

4. Learning Styles: Implications for Improving Educational Practices
   Charles S. Claxton and Patricia H. Murrell

5. Higher Education Leadership: Enhancing Skills through Professional Development Programs
   Sharon A. McDade

6. Higher Education and the Public Trust: Improving Stature in Colleges and Universities
   Richard L. Alfred and Julie Weissman

7. College Student Outcomes Assessment: A Talent Development Perspective
   Maryann Jacobi, Alexander Astin, and Frank Ayala, Jr.

8. Opportunity from Strength: Strategic Planning Clarified with Case Examples
   Robert G. Cope

1986 ASHE-ERIC Higher Education Reports

1. Post-tenure Faculty Evaluation: Threat or Opportunity?
   Christine M. Licata

2. Blue Ribbon Commissions and Higher Education: Changing Academe from the Outside
   Janet R. Johnson and Laurence R. Marcus

3. Responsive Professional Education: Balancing Outcomes and Opportunities
   Joan S. Stark, Malcolm A. Lowther, and Bonnie M.K. Hagerty

4. Increasing Students' Learning: A Faculty Guide to Reducing Stress among Students
   Neal A. Whitman, David C. Spendlove, and Claire H. Clark

5. Student Financial Aid and Women: Equity Dilemma?
   Mary Moran

6. The Master's Degree: Tradition, Diversity, Innovation
   Judith S. Glazer

7. The College, the Constitution, and the Consumer Student: Implications for Policy and Practice
   Robert M. Hendrickson and Annette Gibbs

8. Selecting College and University Personnel: The Quest and the Question
   Richard A. Kaplowitz

1985 ASHE-ERIC Higher Education Reports

1. Flexibility in Academic Staffing: Effective Policies and Practices
   Kenneth P. Mortimer, Marque Bagshaw, and Andrew T. Masland

2. Associations in Action: The Washington, D.C. Higher Education Community
   Harland G. Bloland

3. And on the Seventh Day: Faculty Consulting and Supplemental Income
   Carol M. Boyer and Darrell R. Lewis

4. Faculty Research Performance: Lessons from the Sciences and Social Sciences
   John W. Creswell

5. Academic Program Review: Institutional Approaches, Expectations, and Controversies
   Clifton F. Conrad and Richard F. Wilson

6. Students in Urban Settings: Achieving the Baccalaureate Degree
   Richard C. Richardson, Jr. and Louis W. Bender

7. Serving More Than Students: A Critical Need for College Student Personnel Services
   Peter H. Garland

8. Faculty Participation in Decision Making: Necessity or Luxury?
   Carol E. Floyd

1984 ASHE-ERIC Higher Education Reports

1. Adult Learning: State Policies and Institutional Practices
   K. Patricia Cross and Anne-Marie McCartan

2. Student Stress: Effects and Solutions
   Neal A. Whitman, David C. Spendlove, and Claire H. Clark

3. Part-time Faulty: Higher Education at a Crossroads
   Judith M. Gappa

4. Sex Discrimination Law in Higher Education: The Lessons of the Past Decade*
   J. Ralph Lindgren, Patti T. Ota, Perry A. Zirkel, and Nan Van Gieson

5. Faculty Freedoms and Institutional Accountability: Interactions and Conflicts
   Steven G. Olswang and Barbara A. Lee

6. The High Technology Connection: Academic/Industrial Cooperation for Economic Growth
   Lynn G. Johnson

7. Employee Educational Programs: Implications for Industry and Higher Education*
   Suzanne W. Morse

8. Academic Libraries: The Changing Knowledge Centers of Colleges and Universities
   Barbara B. Moran

9. Futures Research and the Strategic Planning Process: Implications for Higher Education
   James L. Morrison, William L. Renfro, and Wayne I. Boucher

10. Faculty Workload: Research, Theory, and Interpretation
    Harold E. Yuker

1983 ASHE-ERIC Higher Education Reports

1. The Path to Excellence: Quality Assurance in Higher Education
   Laurence R. Marcus, Anita O. Leone, and Edward D. Goldberg

2. Faculty Recruitment, Retention, and Fair Employment: Obligations and Opportunities
   John S. Waggaman

3. Meeting the Challenges: Developing Faculty Careers*
   Michael C.T. Brooks and Katherine L. German

4. Raising Academic Standards: A Guide to Learning Improvement
   Ruth Talbott Keimig

5. Serving Learners at a Distance: A Guide to Program Practices
   Charles E. Feasley

6. Competence, Admissions, and Articulation: Returning to the Basics in Higher Education
   Jean L. Preer

7. Public Service in Higher Education: Practices and Priorities
   Patricia H. Crosson

8. Academic Employment and Retrenchment: Judicial Review and Administrative Action
   Robert M. Hendrickson and Barbara A. Lee

9. Burnout: The New Academic Disease*
   Winifred Albizu Melendez and Rafael M. de Guzmán

10. Academic Workplace: New Demands, Heightened Tensions
    Ann E. Austin and Zelda F. Gamson

*Out-of-print. Available through EDRS. Call 1-800-227-ERIC.

Quantity	Amount

_____ Please send a complete set of the 1989 *ASHE-ERIC Higher Education Reports* at $80.00, 33% off the cover price.   _____

_____ Please begin my subscription to the 1990 *ASHE-ERIC Higher Education Reports* at $80.00, 41% off the cover price, starting with Report 1, 1990   _____

_____ Outside the U.S., add $10 per series for postage   _____

Individual reports are avilable at the following prices:

1990 and forward, $17.00	1983 and 1984, $7.50
1988 and 1989, $15.00	1982 and back, $6.50
1985 to 1987, $10.00	

Book rate postage within the U.S. is included. Outside U.S., please add $1 per book for postage. Fast U.P.S. shipping is available within the U.S. at $2.50 for each order under $50.00, and calculated at 5% of invoice total for orders $50.00 or above. All orders under $45 must be prepaid.

PLEASE SEND ME THE FOLLOWING REPORTS:

Quantity	Report No.	Year	Title	Amount

Subtotal:	
Foreign or UPS:	
Total Due:	

Please check one of the following:
☐ Check enclosed, payable to GWU-ERIC.
☐ Purchase order attached ($45.00 minimum).
☐ Charge my credit card indicated below:
  ☐ Visa   ☐ MasterCard

Expiration Date _____

Name _____

Title _____

Institution _____

Address _____

City _____ State _____ Zip _____

Phone _____

Signature _____ Date _____

SEND ALL ORDERS TO:
ASHE-ERIC Higher Education Reports
The George Washington University
One Dupont Circle, Suite 630
Washington, DC 20036-1183
Phone: (202) 296-2597